TRANSLATIONS FROM GREEK AND ROMAN AUTHORS

Series Editor: GRAHAM TINGAY

HERODOTUS
The Persian War

Translated by WILLIAM SHEPHERD

CAMBRIDGE
UNIVERSITY PRESS

CAMBRIDGE UNIVERSITY PRESS
Cambridge, New York, Melbourne, Madrid, Cape Town, Singapore, São Paulo, Delhi

Cambridge University Press
The Edinburgh Building, Cambridge CB2 8RU, UK

Published in the United States of America by Cambridge University Press, New York

www.cambridge.org
Information on this title: www.cambridge.org/9780521281942

First published 1982
Fourth printing 1998
Re-issued in this digitally printed version 2008

A catalogue record for this publication is available from the British Library

ISBN 978-0-521-28194-2 paperback

Maps by Reg Piggott

Cover: There the Greeks fought on against the Persians with their swords, those that still had them, and with their bare hands and with their teeth.' (See p.60.) The illustration shows a Greek hoplite warrior attacking a Persian foot soldier. It is reproduced by courtesy of the Royal Scottish Museum, Edinburgh.

Contents

Greece and the Western Persian Empire

Land over 1000 m

0   50 miles

0   50   100 km

MACEDONIA

R. Strymon

Abdera

Therma

Thasos

PIERIA

Acanthus Canal

Olynthus

Potidaea

Athos

TEMPE

R. Peneus

Casthanea

THESSALY

Pagasae

C. Sepias

Alus

Aphetae

Sciathos

Artemisium

A e g

MALIS

Trachis

Thermopylae

EUBOEA

Eripus

LOCRIS

Delphi

Chalcis

Eretria

Thebes

Plataea

Marathon

Megara

Carystus

Sicyon

Athens

Corinth

ATTICA

Phlius

Mycenae

Salamis

Andros

Tegea

Argos

Aegina

Troezen

PELOPONNESE

LACEDAEMON

Sparta

Cythera

1   Greece and the western Persian empire

Introduction

HERODOTUS AND HISTORY

Herodotus was born in Halicarnassus, a Greek city of the Persian empire, between 490 and 480 B.C. He was born at the time of the great conflict between the Greeks and the Persians of which he was to write the history. He died at the age of fifty-five or sixty. Herodotus travelled widely, perhaps because he had trading interests, and he was an obsessive collector and teller of stories. The travelling and the writing must have begun early in his life, taking him north into the Black Sea, south to Egypt, east to Tyre and perhaps even to Babylon, and west to Thurii in Italy. Herodotus was a very cosmopolitan Greek and in these travels Athens was more of a base than Halicarnassus.

The subject of Herodotus' story-collecting and writing became 'the great and noble deeds of both Greeks and barbarians', and his purpose 'to record them and preserve their memory and, in particular, to set down the causes of the war between the Greeks and the barbarians'. Herodotus was not the first historian of the Greek world, but his superiority is shown by the fact that his work has been preserved in its entirety, whereas almost nothing survives of the writings of his predecessors and contemporaries. Thucydides, who was born only twenty-five years after Herodotus, was, by modern standards, superior in both historical technique and historical judgement. As a historian, Thucydides stood on Herodotus' shoulders. Herodotus had no comparable support.

The Greek word *historia* from which our word 'history' is derived can be translated most accurately as 'enquiry' or 'research'. Herodotus was a great asker of questions. Few of the answers he needed could be found in written sources so he had to talk to people and rely on their memories and oral traditions. He was a good listener, certainly, good at remembering and recording what he heard. Where his facts can be tested against other sources, they often prove surprisingly accurate. If he confused questions like 'What happened?', 'How did it happen?' or 'Who did it?' with the more fundamental question, 'Why did it happen?', this is because nobody had yet learned to think about causes and effects in a more structured way.

Herodotus can be accused of gullibility and prejudice, or inability to detect bias in his sources. Often he may have been satisfied by only one account of a particular event when inconsistencies, obvious

RB

lapses of memory or blatant ignorance cried out for cross-checking. But this, too, is to accuse him of failing to use an intellectual process that was only just developing in the Greek mind. There is evidence – the occasional incredulous aside or the conscious weighing of one point of view or account against another – that Herodotus' own mind was developing in this way.

Seen in the context of the rapidly changing and turbulent world in which he was writing, Herodotus' *History* is a monumental achievement. In fact, by any standards it is a monumental achievement! The necessary historical questions are not as systematically asked or or answered as modern historians would desire. The 'great and noble deeds' are sometimes hopelessly entangled with 'the causes'. But, as far as the war itself is concerned, most of the questions and most of the answers are there, and much more besides.

THE PERSIANS

Most of the first half of Herodotus' *History* (Books 1–5), over 300 pages of it in a full-length text, is an account of the growth of the Persian empire. This account is supported by detailed descriptions of the many races and lands that became a part of the empire in an astonishingly short time. Persia was ruled in that period by three great warrior kings – first Cyrus, then Cambyses and, after Cambyses, Darius.

Under Cyrus, in the middle of the sixth century B.C., the Persians burst out of their relatively small mountain home north of the Persian Gulf and conquered Media and Lydia. At this time some Greeks, too, became Persian subjects. These were Greeks who had come from mainland Greece in the previous century and colonised islands and coastal land on the eastern side of the Aegean Sea, in an area which came to be known as Ionia. Shortly afterwards, Cyrus added the kingdom of Babylon to his empire. On his death he was succeeded by Cambyses, his son. Cambyses added Cyprus, Egypt, Syria and Phoenicia to the Persian empire. The Phoenicians were sea-traders like the Greeks and they had a large navy.

The Greeks had attempted to resist the Persians in Ionia. Because there were trading connections, formal alliances or ties of kinship between the Greeks of Ionia and the Greeks of the mainland, Greece and Persia were enemies. With control of the powerful Phoenician navy, the Persian empire became a very direct threat to the islands and mainland cities of Greece. In any case, since the Persian empire now extended far into North Africa, the next push westwards was almost certain to carry it into Europe.

Cambyses was succeeded by Darius, his cousin. Darius organised

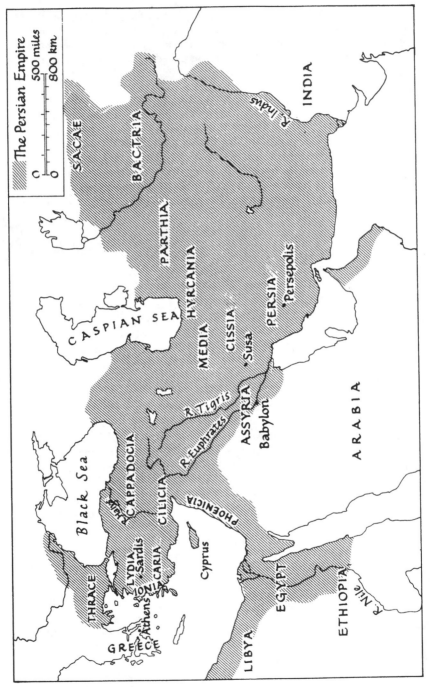

2 The Persian empire in 480

the empire into twenty provinces, which were ruled by *satraps*. These governors were always of noble birth and usually Persian. They were directly responsible to the Great King for the administration of their provinces, the collection of taxes, the raising of troops for the imperial army and for the well-being of all the people under their rule. Roads linked all parts of the empire and provided the King with an efficient communications network and his subject nations with a valuable system of trade-routes. Darius extended the empire as far east as the river Indus and led the inevitable first expedition across the Hellespont into Europe. Leadership, ruling and conquest were the King's divine duty and Darius was more than equal to the demands of his position. He could proclaim with pride that was entirely justified,'I am one King of many, one Lord of many, the Great King, King of Kings, Ruler of the Lands, of all kinds of peoples, King of this great earth far and wide.'

The Greeks called the Persians *barbaroi* – 'barbarians'. They did not mean by this that the Persians were wild savages, but simply that they babbled in a language nothing like Greek. And the Persians were certainly not barbarians in our sense of the word. They were good fighters and hunters, tough and straightforward. But they were also farmers and loved gardens, trees and rivers. They were good organisers and administrators, and natural leaders. Their empire was, by contemporary standards, humane and liberal, as long as their subjects showed themselves content to remain subjects. Trade flourished within it and around it, although the Persians were not traders themselves; they used the empire to amass wealth but put the wealth to no productive use. As rulers they were just and tolerant of others' religions and institutions. In return for the payment of tribute and the acceptance of their sovereignty, they guaranteed their subjects a degree of prosperity and stability which they would not otherwise have enjoyed. Finally, the Persians' religion was more highly developed than the Greeks' and influenced the development of other religions in the Near East and of the Greek philosophical movement which had its beginnings in the Greek cities of Ionia. Herodotus clearly felt great admiration for the Persians and their achievements.

THE PERSIAN WAR

The second half of Herodotus' *History* deals with the immediate causes of the war between the Greeks and the Persians and the war itself. This selection begins with Herodotus' account of the 'Ionian Revolt'. The Persian invasion of Greece was a direct consequence of this rebellion of the Greeks in Asia against the Persians. The rebellion must have been due to rather more than the restlessness and ambition of two individuals, Histiaeus and Aristagoras (see pp. 12–14). Equally, the involvement of a small force of Athenians and Eretrians in the burning of Sardis (see pp. 14–15) could not in itself have been sufficient justification for mounting the expeditions of 491 and 490. But if Herodotus makes too much of these two links in the chain of causes and effects that led to the war he mentions incidentally, or at least hints at the larger, underlying reasons.

Herodotus must be closest to the real causes of the Ionian Revolt in the passage on page 16 in which he describes the measures taken by the Persians to secure peace once the rebellion had been put down. But it is likely that these measures did not seem adequate insurance. Was the Persian empire's western frontier likely to remain stable as long as it separated Greek from Greek? Aristagoras' diplomatic mission and its result, though modest, was evidence of the strength of the ties that linked the Greeks on either side of the Aegean. Even though the Persians had replaced tyrannies with democratic governments in their empire, the Ionian Greeks were still tribute-paying subjects. The obvious contrast between the Ionians' situation and the true independence of the democracies of Greece was a source of potentially dangerous tension. This, too, was at a time when democracy and freedom were subjects of great emotional and intellectual concern in the Greek world.

Greece would not bring great extra wealth to the Persian empire or enlarge it significantly, but important trading links would be gained or reinforced. The Persians already had some experience of the effectiveness of Greek hoplite soldiers (see p. 21) and the armies of Greece would add substantially to the empire's military strength. And to the west of Greece there was a much richer target, Sicily and southern Italy.

The Persians knew that the Greeks would be tough opponents in battle. But they were encouraged by the fact that Greece was not a single nation or empire. They would be fighting against an alliance of many small and fiercely independent city states. Some could be bribed, persuaded or frightened into deserting their neighbours; others might be forced apart by rivalry, grudges and the memories of recent wars; in others, the changing will of the people or the replacement of democracy by some other form of government could reverse the decision to fight. The Persians drew confidence from the contrast between their empire and the authority that bound it together, and the apparent fragility of the Greek alliance and the looseness and unpredictability of democratic rule. As Herodotus records, things came very close to turning out as the Persians hoped they would.

From the Persian point of view there were, then, good practical reasons for invading Greece. The history of the next hundred years or more showed that this view was at least partly mistaken – the Persian empire did not grow further, but its stability was not affected by the invasion's ultimate failure. However, any doubts there were about the planned invasion (and Herodotus records how some of these doubts may have been expressed) must have been outweighed by two other forces. Conquest was the Persian's god-given, natural role, and vengeance on the Greeks for their part in the Ionian Revolt would also have been a very powerful motive. It was of practical importance, too, that the Great King should be seen by his subjects to take vengeance.

The Persians' failure to conquer Greece is important because it allowed Greek civilisation, and Athenian civilisation in particular, to flourish in a way it could not have done under Persian rule. If the Greeks had not beaten back the Persians, western civilisation today would be very different and much the poorer. This is why Herodotus' history is so important. It is both part of the intellectual revolution that the Greek victory made possible and by far the fullest and best account available of a crucial moment in the history of the world.

1   The Ionian Revolt

Histiaeus, tyrant of Miletus, had been too successful for King Darius' liking in his activities on Persia's behalf. He had been summoned to the Persian court at Susa and was now being gently but firmly held captive. He was getting restless. Meanwhile Aristagoras, his cousin and brother-in-law, who had been made tyrant of Miletus in his place, was in trouble. He had promised Artaphernes, satrap of Lydia, that he could win the important island of Naxos for the empire if he had Persian support. Artaphernes had given him money, ships and soldiers but the expedition was a failure.

ARISTAGORAS AND HISTIAEUS

Aristagoras was quite unable to keep the promise he had made to Artaphernes. He was under pressure to pay back the money he had borrowed to equip his army, he was afraid of the likely reaction to his failure and he was certain he was going to lose his position as tyrant of Miletus. So he planned a rebellion against the Persians.

Just at this time 'the man with the tattooed head' arrived with a message from Histiaeus in Susa. The message was that Aristagoras should rebel against the King. All the roads were being watched and this was the only way Histiaeus could safely send word: he shaved the head of his most trustworthy slave, tattooed the message on his scalp and waited till the hair had grown again. Then he sent the man to Miletus with instructions to ask Aristagoras to shave his head and read what he saw there. The message was rebellion, as I have said. Histiaeus was tired of being kept at Susa and he sent this message in the hope that he would be sent back to the coast if there was an uprising; if nothing happened at Miletus he thought he had no chance of ever returning there.

All these pressures bore down on Aristagoras at the same time. He discussed the situation with his supporters, told them what he thought about it and revealed Histiaeus' message to them. All agreed with him, urging him to rebel, all except for Hecataeus, the historian, who advised against going to war with the King of the Persians. He listed the nations Darius ruled and described his power but could not persuade the others. So he advised them that the next best plan was to make sure they had command of the sea, but this advice was not taken either.

Aristagoras therefore rebelled openly against the King. His first act, designed to make the Milesians join willingly in the revolt, was to go through the motions of giving up his power as tyrant of Miletus and restoring democracy. He took similar action in the other cities of Ionia.

ATHENS AND SPARTA

Aristagoras travelled to Greece to ask for help and visited Sparta first. According to the Spartans, Aristagoras took a map of the world with him to his audience with their king. It was engraved on a bronze tablet and showed the whole world, the sea and all the rivers. He arrived for his audience and this is what he said. said.

'King Cleomenes, do not be surprised at my eagerness to come here. As I see it, it is shameful that the sons of the Ionians should be slaves and not free men. It is very painful for us and for you above all others, because you are Greece's leading nation. We beg you now, by the gods of Greece, save your Ionian cousins from slavery. You can do this easily. The barbarians are soft, while your courage in war is outstanding. The barbarians fight with bows and short spears. They go into battle in trousers and they wear turbans on their heads. You will beat them easily. Also, there is more wealth in their land than in all the rest of the world. They have gold and silver and bronze; they have beautiful clothes, too, and oxen and slaves. If you want all this, it is yours.'

Aristagoras failed to impress the Spartans with his arguments, in fact they threw him out of the country, so next he went to Athens. The city of Athens had quite recently been freed from tyranny. Harmodius and Aristogeiton had killed Hipparchus, son of Pisistratus, and for four years afterwards the Athenians had suffered tyranny even worse than before under the brother of Hipparchus, Hippias. He was tyrant in Hipparchus' place and, because of his brother's death, hated the Athenians bitterly. The Alcmeonids, an important Athenian family exiled by the Pisistra-tids, tried with other exiles to win their way back by force and free

13

Athens, but they were unsuccessful and suffered considerable losses. Then, so the Athenians say, the Alcmeonids went to Delphi and bribed the priestess to command any Spartan who came to Delphi, whether on a private mission or a public one, to set Athens free. A Spartan army under King Cleomenes had finally driven Hippias and his family out of Athens after thirty-six years of Pisistratid rule.

Then the power of Athens grew and the value of democracy was demonstrated in many ways. Under the rule of tyrants, the Athenians were no better in war than any of their neighbours, but once they were rid of tyranny they became the best by far. Under tyrannical rule they were easily defeated as men are who work for a master rather than for themselves, but once free, every man was eager to achieve great things for himself. At the time of Aristagoras' visit, Athens was the most powerful city in Greece after Sparta.

Aristagoras went before the Athenian assembly and said what he had said in Sparta. He told the Athenians about the wealth of Asia. He told them how the Persians fought, how they used neither long spear nor heavy shield, and how easily they could be defeated. Then he pointed out that the Milesians were settlers from Athens. It was right that Athens, a great power, should come to their rescue. He promised all sorts of things in his anxiety to succeed and finally he won over the Athenians. It seems it is easier to fool a crowd than one man. Aristagoras could not fool one man, Cleomenes the Spartan, but he managed with 30,000 Athenians.

Once persuaded, the Athenians voted to send twenty ships to help the Ionians and these ships started the trouble between the Greeks and the barbarians. Eretria also agreed to send a small force.

THE BURNING OF SARDIS

The Ionian army took the city of Sardis unopposed, all of it except its citadel which Artaphernes himself held with a large force. But the Ionians were unable to loot the city. Most of the houses in Sardis were built of reeds and those that were brick-built had reed roofs. A soldier set one of those houses on fire and the flames spread from house to house over the whole city. With the city burning around them, the Lydians and Persians who were in the citadel streamed down into the market place to the banks of the Pactolus. (This river flows through the middle of the market place and carries gold dust down from Tmolus into the river Hermus and so into the sea.) They were completely hemmed in by the flames and had no other way of escape so they had to come out and fight. Seeing the enemy making a stand, the Ionians were afraid and retreated towards the Tmolus mountains, then made for their ships under cover of darkness. So the city of Sardis was burned and with it the temple of Cybele, the goddess of the land. This gave the Persians their justification for burning the temples of Greece.

The Persians responsible for the territories to the west of the river Halys joined forces and came to the aid of the Lydians. The Ionians were already well away from Sardis but the Persians caught up with them at Ephesus and routed them. Many famous Ionians were amongst those who died. Those who escaped scattered and returned to their cities. After this the Athenians completely abandoned the Ionians in spite of Aristagoras' pleading, but the Ionians pressed on with the war as hard as ever. They were too deeply committed to give up now.

The news that Sardis had been taken and burned by the Athenians and the Ionians was brought to Darius the King, and he was told that Aristagoras the Milesian was behind the conspiracy and had laid the plans. The story goes that when he first heard about this he was not at all concerned about the Ionians. He knew they would not escape punishment for their rebellion, but he asked who the Athenians were. When he had been told he called for his bow. He took it, put an arrow to the string and shot it into the sky, praying as it flew, 'Zeus, grant me revenge on the Athenians.' Then he ordered one of his servants to tell him three times at every meal, 'Lord, remember the Athenians'.

It took the Persians four years to defeat the Ionians. The Ionian alliance finally collapsed at the sea-battle of Lade off Miletus in 494. But Darius did not forget the Athenians.

When the Persians had defeated the Ionians at sea they besieged Miletus, attacking by land and sea, digging mines under the walls and using all kinds of weapon. The city fell, six years after Aristagoras' rising, and the Persians killed most of the men and made slaves of the women and children. The Athenians were full of sorrow at the capture of Miletus. Phrynichus wrote and produced a play called 'The Capture of Miletus' which caused the audience to weep. He was fined a thousand drachmas for reminding the city of this terrible disaster and his play was banned.

That year the Persians made no more war against the Ionians but instead did certain things which greatly benefited the Greeks. Artaphernes, the satrap at Sardis, sent for representatives from all the Ionian cities and made them swear to settle quarrels in the law courts and not to raid each other. He had their land surveyed in *parasangs*, a Persian unit equivalent to three miles (5 km), then set taxes according to these measurements. In fact the level of taxation was much the same as it had been before and has remained the same to the present day. All this brought peace to Ionia.

MARDONIUS' EXPEDITION

In the spring of 492 Mardonius came to the coast to take command of a very large army and fleet. He was a young man and had recently married one of King Darius' daughters. He arrived in Cilicia and sailed with the fleet along the coast of Asia to the Hellespont; other generals led the army there by land. When he reached Ionia, Mardonius did a thing which some Greeks will find very surprising – he removed all the Ionian tyrants and introduced democracy in place of tyranny.

Mardonius then crossed over into Europe with the great fleet and army he had assembled and began to advance on Eretria and Athens. These cities were his final objectives; at least this was the plan that was made public. In fact the Persians intended to overpower as many Greek cities as possible.

The fleet captured Thasos first without the Thasians lifting a hand to prevent it. Then the army made the Macedonians slaves, adding Macedonia to the nations Persia already owned; all the nations to the east of Macedonia were already dominated by Persia. The fleet crossed over from Thasos and sailed along the coast as far as Acanthus, then put out to sea to sail around Athos. While it was sailing round the peninsula a gale blew up from the north. The ships could not ride it out and many were thrown on to Athos. It is said that three hundred ships were wrecked and more than 20,000 men lost their lives. The sea off Athos is full of monsters and these caught and killed some of the men; some were battered to death against the rocks; some could not swim and drowned; some died of cold.

Then a Thracian tribe, the Brygi, made a night attack on the army in their camp in Macedonia, wounding Mardonius and killing many of his men. But the Brygi could not escape Persian slavery. Mardonius did not leave their country until he had defeated them, but after that he had to lead his invasion force home because the Brygi had done so much damage to the army, and the fleet had suffered so severely off Athos. So the Persians went back into Asia. Mardonius' expedition had been a disaster.

2 Marathon

Mardonius' expedition had ended in failure but it had extended the Persian empire westwards, well into Europe along the northern shore of the Aegean. Darius did not intend to abandon his strategy there but immediately planned a second expedition. Like the first one, its final objective was Athens, but the line of approach was to be different. Starting with Naxos, the scene of Aristagoras' failure nine years before and an island well worth winning, the plan was to work through the central Aegean to Euboea and then to Athens. Until the expedition reached Attica various combinations of force, threats of force, diplomacy and subversion met with rapid success.

Hippias, the exiled Athenian tyrant, sailed with the Persians as an adviser. He was now a very old man but had hopes of being returned to power if Athens fell or surrendered. Both he and the Persians hoped that he still had supporters in Athens who could weaken the Athenians' resistance by persuasion or treachery. If the Persians won Athens, they would have a powerful foothold in mainland Greece.

THE SECOND PERSIAN EXPEDITION

Darius wanted to know what the Greeks intended to do: would they fight him or give themselves up? So he sent heralds through all Greece with instructions to demand earth and water as tokens of submission to the King and he also sent heralds to the coastal cities that already paid him tribute. His orders to them were to build warships and horse transports and they began making preparations. Many Greek cities and islands sent earth and water to the King.

Meanwhile Darius was laying his plans. His servant went on reminding him about the Athenians and the Pisistratid exiles kept coming to him with their lies. In any case Darius wanted an excuse to conquer the Greeks who would not send him earth and water. Darius relieved Mardonius of his command because of the failure of his expedition and appointed other generals to lead his army against Athens and Eretria. He put Datis the Mede and Artaphernes, his own nephew and son of Artaphernes the satrap, in command, sending them on their way with orders to conquer the Athenians and the Eretrians and bring them as slaves into his presence.

The newly appointed generals marched to Cilicia in early 490 with a large and well-equipped army. They were joined there by the fleet which had been assembled. The transports ordered by Darius from the cities who paid him tribute arrived too. The horses and army went on board the transports and sailed with six hundred warships to Ionia. From here they did not sail along the coast by way of the Hellespont and Thrace, but instead set course across the Aegean sea from Samos, sailing from island to island. I think they were afraid to sail round Athos on account of the terrible disaster they had suffered there the year before. Besides, Naxos was their first objective. When the Persians arrived the Naxians took to the hills and put up no resistance. The Persians made slaves of everyone they captured and burned the city and its temples, then set sail for the other islands.

At this time the Delians fled from Delos to Tenos. The island of Delos was sacred to Apollo and a very important centre of Greek religion. The Persian fleet approached Delos but Datis sailed ahead and ordered the ships not to anchor there but at Rhenea, the island opposite. He found out where the Delians had gone and sent a herald with this message: 'Holy men, why have you fled? Have you misunderstood my intentions? I have no plans to harm your island, and these are my orders from the King too. Two gods were born here so I will do no harm to the island or the people who live on it. Return now to your homes, therefore, and live on your land.' Datis also made an enormous offering to the gods of three hundred talents worth of frankincense and burned it as a sacrifice on the altar. The Delians were persuaded.

Sailing on from Delos towards Eretria and Athens, the Persians put in at other islands. They raised troops and took the sons of the islanders for hostages but, when they reached Carystus, the Carystians gave no hostages. They also refused to go to war against neighbour cities, meaning Athens and Eretria. So the Persians besieged them and burned their crops, and then the Carystians went over to the Persian side.

When the Eretrians knew that the Persian fleet was sailing to attack them, they begged the Athenians to help them. The Athenians did not refuse; they sent the 4,000 colonists they had settled in the horse-breeding country around Chalcis to help in their defence, but things were in an unhealthy state in Eretria. The Eretrians had sent for help from Athens but they were divided in their intentions. Some advised abandoning the city and taking to the mountains of Euboea, but others, thinking of their own gain, were plotting betrayal to the Persians. However, one of the leading Eretrians discovered both these plans, told the Athenians how things stood and urged them to return home for their own safety. The Athenians followed his advice and saved themselves by crossing over to the mainland.

The Persians sailed for Temenos, Choereae and Aegilea – all towns in Eretrian territory – and captured them. Then they disembarked the cavalry and prepared to attack Eretria itself but the Eretrians decided not to come out and fight. The plan which won the most votes was to defend the walls and stay inside the city.

The Persians attacked fiercely. In six days fighting many died on both sides, then, on the seventh day, two prominent citizens betrayed Eretria. The Persians plundered and burned the temples in revenge for the temples burned at Sardis, and made the people slaves. These were their orders from Darius. They waited a few days after capturing Eretria and then sailed to Attica. They were full of confidence and expected to deal with the Athenians in the same way as they had dealt with the Eretrians. Hippias, the son of Pisistratus, guided them to Marathon, the best part of Attica for cavalry action and not far from Eretria.

As soon as the Athenians knew of their arrival, they marched out to Marathon to meet the Persians. Ten generals led them. One of them was Miltiades, son of Cimon. He had recently come home from the Chersonese and had escaped death twice over. First the Phoenicians had chased him as far as Imbros in their eagerness to capture him and take him to the King. He escaped the Phoenicians and thought he was safely home, but then his enemies at Athens put him on trial, accusing him of ruling as a tyrant in the Chersonese. He escaped again and was then made a general by the people's vote.

Before they left the city the generals sent a messenger to Sparta. He was an Athenian called Phidippides, a champion long-distance runner. When he was in the hills above Tegea he met the god Pan (so he said, and he said it in public in Athens) and Pan called out his name and commanded him to give this message to the Athenians: 'Why do you neglect me? I am your friend. I have often helped you and I will help you in the future.' The Athenians took this message to heart and when things had indeed turned out well for them, they built a temple for Pan below the Acropolis. There they honoured him every year with sacrifices and torch racing.

Phidippides, the general's messenger, reached Sparta the day after he left Athens. He went to the rulers of Sparta and said 'Lacedaemonians, the Athenians need your help. Do not stand by and watch the most ancient city of Greece fall under the power of barbarians. The Eretrians are now slaves and Greece is weakened by the loss of a fine city.' So he delivered his message, as he had been ordered.

The Lacedaemonians decided to send help but they could not act immediately because they did not want to break their law. It was the ninth day of the month and they said they could not march on the ninth day of that month if the moon was not full. So they waited for the full moon and meanwhile, Hippias, the son of Pisistratus, guided the Persians to Marathon.

THE ARMIES

Approximately 10,000 Athenians faced the Persians. Athens' old ally, Plataea, sent its entire force of about 600 men, a courageous and generous act. The Spartans delayed sending help for genuinely religious reasons but came very quickly when their summer festival was over, too late for the battle.

The Athenian battle position was at the southern end of the plain of Marathon and covered the road which led around the coast to Athens. It also sealed off the shorter route to Athens across the hills which provided a useful line of communication but was unsuitable for the movement of large bodies of men. It was a good defensive position across a valley with steep wooded sides to protect its flanks.

Hoplites
The Greeks facing the Persians were *hoplites*, heavily armed footsoldiers. Hoplites carried large, round shields, solidly made of wood and bronze. They had bronze helmets, and bronze greaves to protect their shins and knees, and they wore body armour made of bronze, leather and toughened linen. Their arms and thighs were bare but, compared to Mardonius'

21

troops they were very well protected, especially against the light Asian arrows and javelins. Their main weapon was a heavy thrusting spear about six feet (2m) long. Hoplites also carried short swords with an iron blade of about two feet (55 cm); they only used them if their spears were broken or lost. Hoplite fighting required a high degree of physical fitness and well-drilled discipline, but individual skill in handling weapons was not so important. In battle hoplites stood close together in a line which was normally eight men deep, presenting a solid wall of spears and shields to the enemy. The first two or three rows did the fighting while those behind provided weight and solidity and replaced men in the front ranks as they tired, or were wounded or killed.

The Persian force was larger, possibly considerably larger, than the Athenian force and had two particular strengths: archers and cavalry. But the Persians were more lightly armed than the Greeks and their numerical advantage would not have outweighed this disadvantage in a frontal attack on the Greek hoplites in their strong position. Their best chance would be to catch the Greeks out in the open, on the move and if possible out of formation, and the Athenians knew this. Herodotus gives one reason for the Persians' decision to land at Marathon. Besides being suitable for cavalry action it was far enough away from Athens to give time for the landing to be made unopposed, a particularly important consideration as far as the horses were concerned.

The Athenians could have simply waited behind their city walls. But that would have left the farmland of Attica at the mercy of the Persians. Treachery, in the shape of support for Hippias, was also much more likely to flourish in a besieged city than in an army in the field.

THE BATTLE

The Athenians were in position on some land sacred to Heracles. There they were joined by the Plataeans. Every man in Plataea came to the aid of Athens because the Plataeans had previously made an alliance with the Athenians, who had done a great deal for them.

The Athenian generals were divided. Some were against fighting (they thought they were too few to take on the army of the

Medes), others, Miltiades amongst them, were in favour of it. So the voting was split and the weaker course of action might have been adopted, but there was an eleventh vote – the Polemarch's [the Polemarch was the War Archon, one of ten senior ministers elected by the Athenians each year]. Miltiades went to Callimachus, who was Polemarch at this time, and said, 'Now it depends on you, Callimachus. You can either enslave Athens or you can make her free, leaving a memorial for yourself as long as men live; not even Harmodius and Aristogeiton have such a memorial. For now Athens is in very great danger, the greatest danger the city has ever faced. If Athens surrenders to the Medes, Hippias will return to power but, if Athens survives, she can go on to be the leading city of Greece. Your vote will decide this; we ten generals are equally divided, half for fighting, half against. If we don't fight now, I can see Athens will fall apart – the result will be a sell-out to the Persians. But if we fight no-one can weaken and, if the gods treat us fairly, we can win this battle. The decision is yours; it depends on you. Vote with me and keep our country free; make our city the leading city in Greece. But vote with those who shy away from fighting and you will achieve the exact opposite.'

Callimachus was persuaded. On the Polemarch's vote, the decision was taken to fight. Then the generals who had voted in favour of fighting offered to let Miltiades be commander-in-chief in their places (each general in turn was entitled to the position for a day). However, he did not fight until his own day came round.

On Miltiades' day the Athenian battle line was drawn up with the Polemarch in command of the right flank, according to the Athenian custom of the time, and each of the ten tribes in its usual position, but with the Plataeans on the left of the line. (Ever since, when the Athenians sacrifice at their five-yearly festival, the herald prays for good fortune for Plataea as well as for Athens.) At Marathon the line had to be stretched to make it equal in length to the Persian line; as a result the middle part was only a few ranks deep and weaker than the two flanks which were deeper and up to strength.

The Athenians were in position. The omens were good and the order was given. The two armies were about a mile apart. At a run the Athenians charged the Persians. Seeing them coming at them, the Persians made ready. They thought the Athenians were mad and rushing to certain destruction; they were so few, charging them at the double without cavalry or archers in support – so the Persians thought. But the Athenians got to grips with them all along the line. As far as I know, the Athenians were the first Greeks to charge their enemy at the double; in fact they were the first not to turn and run at the sight of Persian dress and the men who wore it. Before, even the name Persian had been terrifying to Greeks.

The fighting went on a long time. The Persians were positioned in the centre and beat back the Athenians, breaking their line and driving them inland. But on the flanks the Athenians and the Plataeans were winning. The Greeks let the defeated barbarians run, then turned inwards on those who had broken through in the centre and this is how the Athenian victory was won. They cut the Persians down as they ran till they came to the shore. Then they called for torches and tried to prevent the ships being launched.

At this point in the action Callimachus, the Polemarch, was killed fighting bravely. Stesilaus, one of the generals died too. And Cynegirus was killed there, his hand cut off with an axe as he seized a ship's stern. Many other well-known Athenians died then, as well. In the battle about 6,400 barbarians died and 192 Athenians.

The Athenians captured seven ships, but the rest of the Persian fleet got away. The Persians picked up their Eretrian prisoners from the island where they had left them and sailed round Sunium, hoping to win Athens before the Athenians arrived back. There were Athenians who thought the Alcmeonids had plotted this and flashed a signal to the Persians with a shield when they had boarded the ships.

While the Persians sailed round Sunium, the Athenians marched back as quickly as they could to save their city. They arrived first and took up position by the shrine of Heracles at Cynosarges (moving from one plot of land sacred to Heracles, at Marathon, to another). The barbarian fleet anchored for a while off Phaleron, at that time Athens' naval base, then sailed back to Asia.

SOME QUESTIONS

Herodotus' description of the battle of Marathon is not at all detailed and in it he appears to take a lot for granted. This is partly because Marathon became a legend almost immediately, partly because any eye-witness Herodotus may have spoken to would have been very young in 490 and certainly would not have been involved in any planning or decision-making – this applies with almost equal force to Herodotus' account of the years that followed.

In one detail Herodotus was certainly wrongly informed. In 490 the War Archon was not simply 'chairman' of a committee of generals, but elected commander-in-chief of the Athenian army and navy. The extraordinary arrangement described by Herodotus which put Miltiades in command on other generals' 'days' as well as his own need not, therefore, be taken seriously. However, Miltiades' contribution would certainly have been important. He had first-hand knowledge of the Persians from his adventurous years on the fringes of their empire and was an experienced soldier and a natural leader. But Callimachus gave the orders.

Why, then, did the Athenians fight when they did? It made good sense to stay on the defensive and wait for the Spartans, so how did the situation change? One possible explanation is this: the Persians received a message from Hippias' supporters in Athens or simply came to the conclusion that they could not wait any longer and decided to make their move against the city. They left what they considered an ample force to pin down the Athenians at Marathon and cover their embarkation and the rest boarded their ships to sail round the coast to Phaleron. This force, which included the cavalry, was presumably enough to secure Athens but not large enough to land in the face of the victorious hoplites who had hurried round from Marathon.

The Athenians had no option but to begin the battle immediately and could now do so on more even terms. The cavalry was out of the way (a sort of dictionary of Greek quotations published centuries later connects a saying 'the cavalry's away' with the battle of Marathon) and numbers were better balanced. The rapid charge, probably only at a run over about the last 100 yards (100 m) minimised the danger of the Persian arrows. The turning inward of both flanks was a decisive and brilliant move and probably planned in advance. The opposite ends of the line must have been more than half a mile (1 km) apart and hidden from each other by clouds of dust if not by folds in the ground and trees so there could have been no communication between them; a spontaneous movement could not have been well enough co-ordinated to have the effect that was achieved.

The casualty figures are hard to believe although Herodotus is supported by other sources. But through history up to and beyond the battle of Britain there has been a natural tendency for one side to suppress its own losses and exaggerate the other's. At Marathon it seems strange that the Persians lost so many men yet so few ships. Possibly most of the ships were on the way round to Athens and the thousands of Persians who died, according to Herodotus, were trapped between the sea and the Greek spears and shields. But, though less well armed, the Persians would have resisted desperately and it is difficult to imagine how the Greeks killed so many in such a short time with so little loss.

AFTER THE BATTLE

After the full moon 2,000 Spartans came to Athens. They marched so fast that they were in Attica the third day after they left Sparta but they came too late for the battle. All the same, they wanted to look at the Persian dead, so they went on to Marathon and then returned home full of praise for the Athenians and their victory.

I simply cannot believe that the Alcmeonids had an agreement with the Persians or that they signalled with a shield, or that they wanted Athens ruled by the barbarians and Hippias. The Alcmeonids were clearly tyrant-haters. Through their scheming Athens threw off the tyranny of the Pisistratids. It might be argued that they betrayed their country out of hatred for the ordinary people of Athens, but no-one had a better reputation or greater honour in Athens than the Alcmeonids. It simply cannot be that they flashed a shield for such a reason. It cannot be denied that there was a shield signal. It did happen, but whose signal was it? There is no more I can say on the subject.

After the carnage at Marathon, the Athenians thought even more highly of Miltiades – and his reputation had been high before. He asked the Athenians for seventy ships, an army and money. He did not tell them what the aim of his expedition was to be; he just said he would make the Athenians rich if they put him in command. He would lead them to a place where there was much gold to be won without difficulty. This is what he said as he asked for the ships and the Athenians were persuaded and gave them to him. So Miltiades took his army and sailed for Paros. The reason he gave for the expedition was that the Parians had contributed ships to the Persian fleet which came to Marathon. In fact he had a personal grudge against the Parians.

The attack on Paros was a failure. Miltiades was wounded and the Athenian fleet sailed home.

After his return from Paros, Miltiades' name was on everybody's lips. Xanthippus, in fact, had him put on trial for his life before the assembly of the people, charged with the crime of deceiving the people. Miltiades was present at the trial, but he could not defend himself. He had gangrene in his thigh and could only lie there on a stretcher. His friends had to speak in his defence. They reminded the people of the battle of Marathon and his other achievements and the people decided not to sentence Miltiades to death. But he was fined fifty talents for the wrong he had done and soon afterwards the gangrene became worse and he died. His son Cimon paid the fine.

PERSIAN REACTIONS

Darius the King soon heard about the battle of Marathon. He had been very angry with the Athenians on account of the attack on Sardis. Now his anger was even more terrible; he was yet more eager to make war on Greece. He immediately sent messengers to all cities with orders to prepare an army; each city was to provide much more than before – more warships, more horses, more supplies, more transport ships. The King's commands had Asia in a turmoil for three years with the best men being conscripted and equipped for the assault on Greece. But in the fourth year of these preparations the Egyptians rebelled against the Persians. This increased Darius' desire to go to war, against both the Greeks and the Egyptians.

Before the preparations were completed, however, Darius died, after reigning for thirty-six years. He was not able to carry out his plans to punish the Athenians or the rebellious Egyptians. Xerxes, his son, became King in his place. At first he had no enthusiasm for the war on Greece, but prepared the army for an expedition to Egypt. However, his cousin Mardonius, his most influential adviser, had this to say to him, and said it constantly. 'Lord, it is wrong that the Athenians should escape punishment for the great harm they have done Persia. Finish the job you have

27

in hand first; subdue these insolent Egyptians but then march on Athens. It will make you famous and warn the world against attacking your lands.'

He used revenge as his main argument. But he also pointed out that Europe was an excellent place with all sorts of gardens, trees and fine land – no man but the King was fit to own it! Mardonius said all this because he wanted adventure and hoped to be made governor of Greece. And, in time, his arguments succeeded and he persuaded the King to do what he proposed.

In fact other things helped persuade Xerxes. Messengers came from the ruling family in Thessaly, warmly inviting him to come to Greece, and certain Pisistratids came to Susa and gave Xerxes similar encouragement.

3   The eclipse of Greece

Early in Book 7, with two Books to follow, Herodotus begins
his account of Xerxes' invasion of Europe and quickly moves
on to describe the campaigns of 480 and 479, the Persian War
proper.

DEBATE AND DECISION

Herodotus first reconstructs the discussions that led up to
Xerxes' decision to mount this, the third and by far the largest
of the Persian expeditions into Europe, with Greece as the
main objective. Herodotus' reconstruction is undoubtedly
highly imaginative but it is intelligent; Xerxes' speech is the
best statement in the whole *History* of the main reasons for the
Persian invasion of Greece and Europe. Herodotus' sources
would have been Persians whom he met on his travels, and
perhaps also Greeks who had direct or indirect contact with
the Persian court and with the deliberations that took place at
that time. His better sources might have been able to recall
actual phrases and give fairly detailed summaries of what was
said. But for the most part the words must be Herodotus'.
    In his attempt to win Greek support, according to
Herodotus, Aristagoras gave an unbalanced impression of the
Persians' military strength; he stressed how lightly armed they
were, without mentioning their bows and arrows or their
cavalry, their mobility or their great numbers. Mardonius here
stresses the inflexibility of hoplite tactics without considering
the effectiveness of these tactics and hoplite weapons in the
kind of fighting for which they were developed. Artabanus,
Xerxes' uncle, speaks against the invasion and produces even
stronger arguments when he and Xerxes return to the
discussion at Abydos. Artabanus' speeches contribute to
Herodotus' image of Xerxes as a tragic hero rising so high that
his fall becomes inevitable.

Xerxes summoned a council of the leading Persians. His purpose
was to sound out their opinions and let them know his plans. He

addressed them as follows: 'Persians, I am not about to introduce new policy – I am following policy already established. I have learned this from older men; we have never relaxed our efforts since the day Cyrus took power and we won from the Medes the dominating position which is now ours. It is God who leads us – we follow and all the many things we do are successful. You all know what lands Cyrus and Cambyses and Darius, my father, conquered and added to our empire. Since coming to the throne I have been thinking how I am to live up to my predecessors' achievements – I want to add as much to the Persian empire as they did. Now I have thought of a way to win honour and as much land as we now possess, good land and more fertile. At the same time we will get revenge. This is why I have called you together, to tell you my plan.

'I intend to put a bridge across the Hellespont and march an army through Europe into Greece. I am going to punish the Athenians for what they did to Persia and to my father. You know Darius, my father, planned to make war against these men. But he died before he could punish them. Now, for Darius and for Persia, I am not going to rest until I have taken and burned Athens. I will punish the Athenians for the harm they did to my father, and to me too, without provocation. First, they came to Sardis with Aristagoras, our Milesian slave. They burned the sacred groves and the temples. Second, you all know what they did to our forces when they landed in Attica.

'These are my reasons for making war on Athens; and when I think about it, I can see a number of advantages in such an expedition. For if we conquer the Athenians and their neighbours in the Peloponnese, Persian territory will only end where the sky begins. When I have passed through Europe, no land under the sun will be outside our borders. With you I will make all the lands one land. No city or nation, so I have been told, will stand against us in battle – once we have disposed of the Greeks. So those who have wronged us, and the innocent too, will bear the yoke of slavery.'

Mardonius spoke after the King: 'Lord, you are the greatest Persian there has ever been, and ever will be. You have spoken well and what you have said is true. You will not allow the Greeks of Europe to laugh at us – they have no cause to. We are the conquerors and masters of the Sacae, the Indians, the Ethiopians, the Assyrians and many other great nations. They did us no wrong; we simply wanted to add to our empire. It would be a terrible thing if we did not punish the Greeks for injuring us without provocation. What would there be to fear? The size of their army? Their resources? We know the way they fight. We know they have no great strength. Anyway we already have Greeks in our power living on our land, Ionians, Aeolians and Dorians.

'I have tested the Greeks myself. Carrying out your father's orders, I marched as far as Macedonia, nearly as far as Athens. But no Greek came out to meet me in battle. Yet the Greeks do fight wars, I know they do. But their methods are clumsy and hard to make sense of. When war has been declared the two sides find a nice, level patch of ground and fight their battle. The result is that the winners leave the field in very bad shape. But the losers – I can't begin to describe their condition – they are totally wiped out. Yet these people all speak the same language; they should be able to settle their differences by means of ambassadors and heralds, or by any means other than fighting. But if they have to go to war, each side should identify its greatest strength and direct its efforts accordingly. The Greek way is no good and the Greeks certainly didn't think of fighting when I marched as far as Macedonia.

'Who then is going to stand against you, King? You will be at the head of your great host from Asia and all your ships. In my opinion the Greeks won't have the stomach for it but, if I'm proved wrong and they are fools enough to take us on in battle, they will learn we are the best fighters in the world. However, we must concentrate all our efforts; nothing happens automatically, but with effort everything is possible.'

So Mardonius supported Xerxes' proposal with smooth words. The others said nothing. They dared not argue against what had been said. But then Artabanus spoke. He was Xerxes' uncle and so had the courage to speak. 'King, the people you are planning to attack have an excellent reputation as fighters on land and sea. It is my duty to tell you how dangerous they are.

'You say you will bridge the Hellespont and take your army through Europe to Greece. What if you are defeated on land or at sea, or both? These Greeks are said to be great fighters. We already have evidence of this because it was the Athenians on their own who defeated the great army led to Attica by Datis and Artaphernes. If they were to attack and win a battle at sea without a victory on land, they could sail to the Hellespont and break your bridge. Then, King, you would be in great danger.

'You know that God strikes down the great with his thunderbolt and stops their boasting; the lowly are of no concern to him. The tallest buildings and trees are always the ones that he blasts. It is God's way to bring down the mighty. So a great army can be destroyed by a little one.'

Xerxes did not make up his mind immediately. He was impressed by Artabanus' arguments against attacking Greece. But finally both he and Artabanus were persuaded by dreams that the expedition should go ahead and would succeed.

PREPARATIONS

Once Egypt had been reconquered, it took four years to assemble the army and equip it. In the fifth year the King began his march at the head of an enormous force. This army was by far the largest ever recorded. The army Darius led against the Scythians was nothing by comparison. Xerxes' army was also far greater than the one the sons of Atreus led against Troy, according to what we know of that. All the armies of history added together would not have been equal to Xerxes' army. What nation did Xerxes not lead from Asia against Greece? Only the largest rivers could provide his army with water without running dry! Some nations supplied warships, some foot soldiers, some cavalry; some provided horse transports or ships for the bridges and some supplied food.

Because the last attempt to sail round Athos had met with such disaster, preparations there had been going on for three years. A fleet had been based at Elaeus in the Chersonese and from this base detachments were sent across to Athos – men from every race serving in the army. Their task was to dig a canal and they worked in shifts driven on by whips. The people who lived on the peninsula also did some of the digging.

It is my view that Xerxes had this canal built out of pride. He wanted to make a show of his power that would not be forgotten. The Persians could have hauled their ships across the isthmus without difficulty, but Xerxes ordered a channel to be dug for the sea, wide enough for two warships to row through side by side. The men who dug the canal had a further task assigned to them; they were to put a bridge across the river Strymon. The Egyptians and Phoenicians made the rope for the bridges out of papyrus and esparto grass.

At the same time supplies were stockpiled at various points on the route the army was to take. No man or beast would go hungry in the march on Greece. Xerxes had his men look for the best possible places for storing these supplies and they were then shipped over from all parts of Asia.

While these things were being done the whole army assembled at Crytallus in Cappadocia. From there they marched towards Sardis with Xerxes. On the way Xerxes came across a very beautiful plane tree. He decorated it with gold and made one of his personal guard its guardian. When Xerxes reached Sardis, the capital of Lydia, the first thing he did was to send heralds to Greece with demands for earth and water, tokens of submission, and hospitality for the King, but he sent no such demand to Athens or Sparta. He repeated these demands for earth and water because he thought that those who had not given earth and water to Darius the first time would now give it to him through fear. He sent his heralds to check whether he was right about this.

Next, while Xerxes prepared to march to Abydos, some of his men put two bridges across the Hellespont from Asia into Europe. Between the towns of Sestos and Madytus a broad headland runs into the Hellespont opposite Abydos. It is nearly a mile from this headland to Abydos and the bridge builders joined the two places together. One bridge was built with esparto grass rope by the Phoenicians and the other was built by the Egyptians with papyrus.

As soon as the bridges were completed a great storm blew up and broke them, carrying everything away. Xerxes was very angry. He gave orders for the Hellespont to be given three hundred lashes. Also he had fetters thrown into the sea and I have even heard that he sent torturers to brand it with red hot irons. In this way Xerxes had the sea punished. He also had the men in charge of the bridging operation beheaded.

Other engineers started work on the bridges and this is the way they built them. They lashed together ships as pontoons, 360 for the bridge nearer the Black Sea and 314 for the other, positioning them so that the current would put the least strain on the cables. Then they put down heavy anchors to hold the ships against the winds that blow down from the Black Sea, and against the south and west winds that blow from the Aegean. They left openings so that ships could continue to sail up and down the Hellespont. With the pontoons in position they stretched the cables tight using wooden windlasses. This time they did not use one kind of rope on each bridge; each bridge had two cables of esparto and four of papyrus rope. Each kind was of the same thickness and fine appearance, but the esparto rope weighed more.

Next, wooden planks were cut and fitted together over the taut cables. When this decking was fixed in place it was covered with brushwood. This in turn was covered with earth trodden down hard. Finally screens were put up on each side to stop the horses and other animals being frightened by seeing the sea. The bridges were now ready. The canal at Athos was complete, too, with breakwaters at the entrances to stop the sea silting them up.

After wintering in Sardis and making preparations, the army started out for Abydos in early Spring. As the men moved off the sun left its place in the sky. The air was clear and there were no clouds, but day turned into night. This worried Xerxes and he asked the Magi what the vision meant. They told him that God's message was the eclipse of the cities of Greece. They said that the sun told the future for the Greeks but the moon told the future for the Persians. This interpretation delighted Xerxes and he pressed on with the expedition.

Pythius the Lydian was terrified by the eclipse. His five sons were in the army and he begged Xerxes to let the eldest stay behind. Xerxes was very angry at this. He ordered his executioners to find Pythius' eldest son and cut him in two, then put half his body on each side of the road the army was to march on. Xerxes' order was carried out and the army marched off between the two halves.

The time the Persians spent in preparation for the invasion may be exaggerated but it was certainly a major operation and very well organised. The canal through the Athos peninsula does seem a rather extravagant gesture but the bridge building and the stockpiling of supplies, and the evident thoroughness of the planning are highly impressive. The effect of this activity on all but the most determined and best protected Greeks was predictable. If this section ends with two episodes that seem barbaric in the modern sense, it is worth noting that the Magi had a better than primitive understanding of eclipses and that the Greeks were also capable of acts of barbarism and savagery. It has been calculated that there was an eclipse of the sun which could have been observed by Xerxes but it took place about a year earlier, in the spring of 481. Herodotus' timing of the eclipse is more dramatic.

ABYDOS

When he arrived at Abydos, Xerxes wanted to review his entire force. The people of Abydos, acting on the King's orders, had already built him a throne of white stone on a hill for this purpose. There he sat looking down towards the sea at his army and his fleet, and as he looked them over he thought he would like to see his ships race. The Phoenicians of Sidon won and Xerxes was pleased by the racing and by his army. But when he saw the whole Hellespont covered with his ships and the plains of Abydos filled with his troops, first Xerxes thought himself the luckiest of men, then he wept.

Artabanus, seeing Xerxes weep said 'King, how different what you are doing now is from what you did a moment before. You called yourself happy and now you weep.'

Xerxes replied 'I suddenly thought how short human life is, and I was filled with pity. Not one of those men there will be alive in a hundred years' time.' Xerxes then had a question for Artabanus. 'If you had not had that clear vision in your dream, would your opinion now be the same as it was before? Would you still stop me going to war against Greece, or would you now have changed your mind? Tell me the truth.'

Artabanus answered 'King, I pray that the vision I saw in my dream turns out to be true as we both wish. But since that vision I have been full of dread for many reasons. Most of all I fear to see you face the two greatest enemies of all.'

Xerxes replied 'My dear fellow, what are these, my two greatest enemies? Is our army too small? Will the Greek army be many times greater? Is our fleet too small, or is the fault with both? If our forces are less than we need, we can quickly raise more.'

Artabanus answered 'King, no sensible man would criticise your army or the size of your navy. But, if you add to your forces, the two enemies I am speaking of will become greater still. These two enemies are land and sea.

'To my knowledge there isn't a harbour anywhere large enough to shelter your fleet in a storm and keep it safe. And it isn't one harbour you need – you need harbours all along the coast you will be sailing down. But there isn't one and you must learn that disasters control men; men do not have control over disasters. And I will tell you about the land, your other enemy. If you meet with no opposition, the land will become a greater

35

enemy the further you advance. You won't think what lies ahead – no man is ever satisfied if he is successful – so, if nobody resists you, I tell you, you will add to your lands but starvation will follow in time.'

Xerxes' reply was this: 'Great prizes are won by taking great risks. We will do as our fathers did. We are campaigning at the best time of year and we will return home, conquerors of Europe. We will not suffer famine or any other disaster. For we march with plentiful supplies and we shall also have the produce of whatever lands we conquer to live on. We are marching against farmers, not nomads.'

Xerxes then sent for the noblest of the Persians. They came, and he addressed them in these words: 'Persians, I have called you here to tell you what I require of you. You must fight with courage and you must not disgrace the glory of the great past achievements of the Persians. Each and every one of us must do his utmost for the best advantage of all. I urge you to give everything in this war, for I hear the men we will be fighting are brave. If we defeat them, no other human army will ever stand against us.

'Now let us pray to the gods who watch over Persia – then let us cross.'

All that day the Persians prepared for the crossing. Then they waited to see the next day's sun rise and burned all kinds of incense and spread branches of myrtle on the road. At sunrise Xerxes poured an offering into the sea from a golden flask and prayed to the sun that no misfortune would prevent him conquering Europe or turn him back before he reached its furthest boundaries. After praying he threw the flask into the Hellespont with a golden bowl and a Persian short sword. I cannot be certain myself if he threw these things into the sea as an offering to the sun; maybe he regretted having the sea whipped and gave the gifts to the Hellespont to make up for it.

After this the crossing began. The foot soldiers and cavalry crossed by the bridge nearer the Black Sea. The baggage train used the other bridge. The Persian Ten Thousand were the first to cross, all wearing garlands, and they were followed by a mixed force of troops from every nation. This took all that first day. Next day the cavalry crossed first, followed by another contingent of Persians carrying spears and wearing garlands. Then came the sacred horses and chariot and then Xerxes himself with a thousand horsemen and a thousand spearmen. The rest of the army followed and at the same time the fleet rowed to the opposite shore. I have also heard that the King crossed over last of all, however.

Mardonius and five other generals were in overall command of the land army except for the Ten Thousand. Hydarnes was commander of this corps of specially picked Persians. They were known as the Immortals because they were never more or less than ten thousand; if a man died or fell sick another was immediately chosen in his place.

The Persians were the best troops in the army and looked the most magnificent, equipped as I will describe. They also had large amounts of gold which they lavishly displayed and they brought their women and servants with them by the wagon load. Camels and other transport animals carried their food, separate from the rest of the army's supplies. The Persian cavalry were equipped in the same way as the Persian foot soldiers but some of them wore helmets of hammered bronze or iron.

After he had crossed into Europe Xerxes watched the army marching over under the lash. Seven days and seven nights the army took to cross, without a moment's pause. There is a story that, when Xerxes had completed the crossing, a man who lived by the Hellespont said 'Zeus, why take the shape of a Persian and change your name to Xerxes? Why lead the whole world behind you, if you want to uproot Greece? You could easily do it without any help!'

XERXES' ARMY AND FLEET

Herodotus' numbers, based firmly on tradition, are incredible if not impossible. The grand total he eventually arrives at is more appropriate to a population movement than to a military operation. Herodotus was probably working from information about the full potential military strength of the Persian empire at about that time. It must have seemed entirely appropriate for Xerxes to take his entire army and navy with him to Greece (regardless of the needs of the rest of the empire). Besides, the tradition of tens of thousands of Greeks heroically resisting thousands upon thousands of barbarians was sacred. Herodotus' duty was to document this tradition, not to challenge it.

When the Persians reached central and southern Greece it seems certain that they significantly outnumbered any army or

37

fleet that the Greeks could put in the field against them. But the battles that were fought and the way they were fought strongly suggest that the Persians had nothing like the force that tradition provides them with. A reasonable estimate is that around 200,000 men marched into Europe; detachments would have been left behind at each important stage, but Greek troops were also drafted in as the advance progressed. Similarly, the Persian fleet may not, in fact, have been overwhelmingly larger than the Greek; a reasonable estimate of its numbers might be 600 warships.

It is possible that all the nations of the Persian empire were represented in the invasion force but a number of them may only have provided token contingents led by high-ranking generals or princes; their main function may have been as hostages to guarantee good behaviour at home in the King's absence.

On reaching Doriscos Xerxes counted his troops. I cannot say precisely how many there were in each detachment; no-one has kept a record of that, but the complete land army totalled 1,700,000 men. This is how they were counted: ten thousand men were assembled in one place and packed as closely together as possible. Then a line was drawn round them and a wall was built about waist high. The rest of the troops were marched through this enclosure until the whole army had been counted.

The following nations served in the army. First of all there were the Persians. They were equipped as follows: they wore felt caps, long-sleeved brightly coloured tunics, fine iron mail that looked like fish scales, and trousers. They carried wicker shields with quivers beneath them, short spears, long bows with reed arrows and short swords hanging from their belts against their right thighs. They were commanded by Otanes, the father of Xerxes' wife. The Medes were equipped in the same way; in fact this style of dress and equipment is Median not Persian. Tigranes, also a relation of the king, commanded the Medes. The Cissians were also equipped like the Persians, but they wore turbans instead of felt caps. Their commander was Anaphes, the son of Otanes.

The Bactrians in the army wore headgear similar to the Medes', but they carried the reed bows of their country and short spears. The Sacae from Scythia wore tall, pointed hats and trousers. They carried their own kind of bow and a dagger and a special kind of battle axe. The Sacae and the Bactrians were commanded by Hystaspes, son of Darius. The Indians were dressed in cotton and their weapons were reed bows and arrows tipped with iron.

Herodotus mentions and describes the Hyrcanians, the Assyrians, the Arabians, the Ethiopians, the Libyans, the Phrygians, the Lydians and the Thracians and several other contingents. However, none of these are mentioned again in the battles that were fought in Greece. He also names several other nations that provided cavalry, for which he gives a total number of 80,000, and mentions that the army included chariots and camels.

For the fleet Herodotus gives a total number of 1,207 *triremes* (see page 66). Smaller warships and transports bring this total up to a colossal 3,000. 300 of the triremes were Phoenician and 200 Egyptian. The next largest contribution, 150 triremes, came from Cyprus and then Cilicia, the Ionian Greeks and the Hellespont area each contributed 100. The balance was made up of smaller forces from other maritime subject states. In his descriptions of the two sea-battles of 480 Herodotus only specifically mentions about half of the dozen major naval forces he lists earlier in the *History*.

DAMARATUS

Damaratus, one of Sparta's two joint kings, had been unfairly deposed by Cleomenes, his fellow king, some years earlier. He accompanied Xerxes as an adviser and there were probably plans for him to rule again in Sparta under the Persians once Greece was conquered. Herodotus does not seem to consider him a traitor; indeed he tells how Damaratus sent a secret message warning Sparta that the invasion was imminent. Herodotus uses his 'conversations' with Xerxes to comment pointedly and effectively on the main narrative.

After reviewing the army and the fleet Xerxes summoned Damaratus to him and said, 'Now tell me this. Will the Greeks stand fast and lift a hand against me? I do not think so. Even if all the Greeks and everyone else who lives further west join forces, they could not stand against me in battle, and they are not united anyway. But I would like to know what you think.'

'Do you want a true answer or one that will please you?' Damaratus asked. Xerxes told him to speak the truth and assured him that he would not lose favour by doing so.

Damaratus then said 'King, I think highly of all Greeks. But I will only tell you about the Spartans. First, they will never accept from you terms that bring slavery to Greece. Second they will take you on in battle even if all other Greeks give in. Don't ask me about numbers. No matter how small it is, the Spartan army will fight you.'

Xerxes laughed 'What a thing to say! If they were under the rule of one man, the Persian way, they would excel themselves for fear of that man. Driven by the lash they might fight on, though outnumbered, but given the freedom to choose, your Spartans wouldn't do either of these things. You are talking nonsense.'

'King, I knew you wouldn't like the truth,' Damaratus replied. 'In single combat a Spartan is as good as any man. Fighting together, Spartans are the best on earth. They are free, but not absolutely free. They have a ruler, the law. They fear the law much more than your men fear you. They do what the law commands. And one thing it always commands – never run away in battle whatever the odds; stand firm and win, or die. If you think I am talking nonsense, I will say no more. I am saying this because you make me say it. I hope everything turns out as you think it should, King.'

Xerxes just laughed and was not at all annoyed by Damaratus' answer.

4   Face your doom!

Half way through Book 7 Herodotus turns his attention to the
Greeks and their reactions to Xerxes' preparations and
advance. Earth and water, the symbols of submission, were
sent to the King by many cities of northern and central
Greece. Thebes, only thirty miles (50 km) from Athens as the
crow flies, was one of them. As the later actions of the
Thessalians and Thebans show, the sending of earth and water
was not considered to be a binding commitment, but it was at
least evidence of a rather lukewarm concern for the fate of
Greece. Those Greeks who were determined to resist began to
look for support, from men and from the gods.

GREEK REACTIONS

Xerxes spent a number of days in Pieria. A third of the army was
clearing a road through the highlands of Macedonia to make a
route for the rest. During this time the heralds that had been sent
into Greece to demand earth and water began to arrive back.
Some came empty handed, some returned with the tokens of submission. Amongst those who sent earth and water were the
Thessalians, the Locrians, the Magnesians, the Melians, the
Thebans and all the cities of Boeotia except for the Thespians
and the Plataeans.

The Greeks who had decided to fight against the Persians
swore an oath. They would dedicate to the god at Delphi a tenth
of the possessions of all the Greeks who had given in to the Persians without being forced. This they swore to do if they won the
war. Xerxes sent no heralds to Athens or Sparta because of what
happened when Darius had demanded earth and water before.
The Athenians had thrown the heralds in a pit (the one they
threw condemned criminals into) and the Spartans had thrown
them down a well and told them to get earth and water for the
King from there.

Although the main objective of Xerxes' expedition was said to
be Athens, his real target was the whole of Greece. The Greeks

41

had been aware of this for some time, but they did not all react in the same way. Those who had submitted to the Persians were confident that they would suffer no harm. But the others were very frightened. There did not seem to be enough ships in Greece to take on the invaders and most Greeks did not want to get involved in the war and were going over to the Persian side without hesitation.

ATHENS AND THE DELPHIC ORACLE

The almost defiant warning with which Herodotus opens this section must be understood in the context in which it was written – Athens by then had an empire, many enemies and few friends. This reminder of Athens' vital part in the Persian War would have been unpalatable to many of Herodotus' readers who now resented, felt threatened or were dominated by the same naval power that had saved them from becoming part of the Persian empire.

The Greeks believed that the gods communicated with them through oracles. They took oracles very seriously and consulted them about both personal and public matters. Apollo's oracle at Delphi was the most important oracle and a mission to Delphi would have been a vital part of the Athenians' preparation for war.

The priestess of the Delphic oracle, the Pythia, delivered Apollo's messages in a deep trance. The words she spoke were interpreted and written down for enquirers by other priests and priestesses who attended her and important decisions could be influenced by them. Delphi was a holy place, but it was also a centre of financial and political influence. Some of Apollo's utterances through the Pythia were interpreted to serve earthly purposes. The right answers could be bought on occasion, and, like statistics and opinion polls today, oracles could be used as a political tool. The first answer given to the Athenians is an example of this; it seems that the Delphians thought their future would be more secure within the Persian empire, especially if they could claim to have helped the Persians by persuading the Athenians to abandon Greece. The intensity of the Athenians' appeal for a better answer perhaps aroused a stronger sense of religious duty and patriotism.

At this point I feel I must express an opinion which many readers will not like; all the same I shall not let that stop me saying what I think is the truth. If the Athenians had abandoned their country for fear of the danger approaching, or if they had stayed and surrendered to Xerxes, no-one would have tried to resist the King on the sea.

With no resistance at sea this is what would have happened on land: the Spartans would have been deserted by their allies, even if the Peloponnesians had built many walls across the Isthmus for their protection. The allies would have been compelled to desert them as their cities were picked off one by one by the Persian fleet. The Spartans would finally have been isolated and, standing alone, would have done great deeds and died splendid deaths. Alternatively, seeing the rest of Greece going over to the Persians, they would have come to an agreement with Xerxes. Either way, Greece would have come under Persian rule. I cannot see that fortifying the Isthmus would have been any use if the King had control of the sea.

Anyone who says that the Athenians saved Greece, then, is absolutely right. The Athenians could have tipped the balance, whichever way they turned, and they chose that Greece should remain free. It was the Athenians who roused the other Greeks to action – those who had not sided with the Persians. It was the Athenians, after the gods, who beat back the King. The alarming prophecies that came from Delphi terrified the Athenians but they would not desert Greece. They stood fast and faced up to the invader.

The Athenians had sent ambassadors to Delphi asking for a prophecy from the oracle. When the ambassadors had performed the usual rites they went into the inner chamber and took their places. The priestess gave them this answer:

'Why do you wait, Athenians? There is no hope for you.
Fly to the ends of the earth.
Leave your homes; leave your city,
The high citadel and its circling walls.
Neither head nor body
Nor feet nor hands will stand fast.
Nothing will be left, only disaster.
Fire and fierce Ares, driving a Syrian chariot,
Will wreck your city, and other strongholds too.
Flames will devour your holy temples.
Even now they stream with sweat and quake with fear;
Dark blood runs from the roof tiles.

They foresee calamity inescapable.
Go, therefore, leave! Face your doom with courage.'

Hearing this, the Athenian ambassadors were very distressed.
The disaster which had been prophesied almost made them
abandon hope. But someone advised them to take olive
branches and go again to the oracle, begging for a second
prophecy. This they did and said, 'Lord Apollo, look kindly
on these olive branches and give us a better answer about our
country's fate. If you do not, we shall not leave your temple;
we shall stay here till we die.'
    Then the priestess prophesied a second time:

> 'Pallas Athene cannot sway the will of Zeus
> With words of prayer or clever argument.
> But a second answer I will give you.
> Cecrops' land and the valleys of holy Cithaeron will be
>   taken.
> But far-seeing Zeus grants Athens this:
> Only a wooden wall will keep you safe,
> A safe keep for you and your children.
> Stay not for the mighty army coming from the north,
> The mighty army covering the land with horse and foot.
> Retreat, turn your back! Yet you will meet in battle.
> Blessed island, Salamis, you will be the death of mothers'
>   sons
> At seedtime or at harvest time.'

This seemed a better answer than the first – and indeed it
was – so the ambassadors wrote it down and returned to
Athens. On arrival they read it out before the people. Many
different interpretations were offered and two in particular
stood out. Some of the older men thought the god meant that
the acropolis would hold out. Their argument was that the
acropolis had been fenced with thorn in the past and that the
'wooden wall' referred to this fence. But others said the god
was talking about the navy and urged that all efforts should
be concentrated on making it ready. But this second group
could not make sense of the last lines of the answer. These
words seemed to run right against the interpretation that
'wooden wall' meant ships. In fact the experts took the lines
to mean that the Athenians would attempt a sea-battle off
Salamis, but that they would be defeated.

THEMISTOCLES

There was one Athenian who interpreted these last lines differently. His name was Themistocles and he had recently risen to a position of prominence. This Themistocles said that the experts had interpreted the answer wrongly. He argued that harsher words would have been used if an Athenian disaster had been foretold. The words would have been 'wretched island' not 'blessed island' if disaster was in store for whoever was based there. The correct interpretation was that the oracle meant death for the enemies of Athens, not the Athenians. Themistocles, then, advised the Athenians to prepare to fight at sea. Their navy was to be their wooden wall.

The Athenians preferred Themistocles' advice and rejected the expert interpretations. The experts were against fighting at sea, in fact they did not want Athens to lift a hand against the invaders. They were for leaving Attica and finding somewhere else to live.

On a previous occasion Themistocles' opinion had persuaded the Athenians to make an important decision. This was when the treasury had received a large sum in extra revenue from the silver mines at Laurium. The intention had been to divide this equally amongst all the citizens of Athens, each receiving ten drachmas. But Themistocles persuaded the Athenians not to do this but instead to use the money to build two hundred ships for the war they were fighting at the time against Aegina. Flaring up then, that war saved Greece by making seamen of the Athenians. Those ships were not actually used for the war for which they were built, but the Athenians had them ready when Greece needed them, and they had to build more as well.

After discussing the oracle's message, the Athenians decided to do what the god said. They would meet the invader with their ships, with every man they could muster and with all the Greeks who would join them.

Athens was the key nation in the defence of Greece and
Themistocles was the key man in Athens. Herodotus' sources,
and possibly Herodotus himself, had very mixed feelings about

Themistocles. His policy of building up the Athenian navy had resulted in a reduction of the political power of the great families and the richest citizens generally. This came about because the ordinary citizens who built and rowed the ships grew in confidence and political importance. They were the bedrock of Themistocles' own power and with their support he was amongst Athens' most prominent citizens for over twenty years. There were powerful Athenians who could not forgive Themistocles for the changes they held him responsible for and Herodotus must have talked to many of them.

However, Herodotus appears to have more conviction when he writes what seems to be the truth about Themistocles than when he records what is less to his credit and often less likely. A little later in Book 7 he writes, 'My task is to tell you what people tell me, but I don't have to believe it.' This needs to be remembered throughout the *History*. It is a pity he does not tell us what he thinks more often!

THE GREEK ALLIANCE

All who cared about the good of Greece met in conference, promised loyalty to each other and agreed to put an end to all disputes and wars amongst themselves. At the time there were a number of these going on, but the most serious was the war between Aegina and Athens.

The allies were informed that Xerxes was in Sardis with his army. They decided to send spies into Asia to find out about the King's preparations. They sent ambassadors to Argos hoping to make the Argives their allies against Persia and also sent messages to Gelon, the most powerful Greek ruler in Sicily, to Corcyra and to Crete. It was hoped that all Greece could be united in this one cause, since the danger threatened all those of Greek blood.

These decisions were taken and all disputes were settled. Then three men were sent to Asia to spy. They went to Sardis and managed to learn a good deal about the King's army, but they were caught. The Persian generals questioned them and then sent them off to be executed. Xerxes heard that they had been sentenced to death and was not pleased with the generals' decision. He sent some of his personal guard with instructions to bring the spies to him, if they were still alive. They were still alive and so were brought into the King's presence. He asked them why they had come, then commanded that they be shown the whole army, both foot soldiers and cavalry. They were to see all they wanted to see and then leave unharmed for any country they chose.

The reason the King gave for his command was this: 'If the spies had been put to death, the Greeks would not hear so soon how tremendous my forces are. Besides, killing three men would not have harmed the enemy much. But once the spies reach home and say what they have seen, the Greeks may decide to give up their liberty before the expedition even begins. So we may not need to invade Greece at all!'

Xerxes had said something similar on another occasion. When he was at Abydos he saw corn ships sailing down the Hellespont from the Black Sea with cargoes for Aegina and the Peloponnese. His staff realised these were enemy ships and wanted to capture them. They turned to Xerxes expecting him to give the orders and the King asked 'Where are they sailing?'

'To your enemies, King, carrying corn,' they said.

Xerxes replied, 'Are we not sailing in the same direction, carrying corn amongst other things? What harm are these ships doing transporting corn for us?'

> The people of Argos, the Cretans, the Corcyreans and the Sicilians sent no help. Herodotus gives various reasons. It seems that the Argives were unwilling to fight in an army commanded by Sparta, their old enemy. The Corcyreans either did not want to get involved or unfavourable winds held their fleet up. The Cretans were instructed not to fight by the Delphic oracle, or so they claimed. Gelon of Syracuse in Sicily was also reluctant to put his army under Spartan command. In any case the Carthaginians invaded Sicily that year, so it may have been impossible for the Sicilian Greeks to send help. The Carthaginian invasion of Sicily and the Persian invasions of Greece may even have been co-ordinated.

NORTHERN GREECE

The Thessalians sided with the Persians at first, but unwillingly. One of the leading Thessalian families had arranged this against the will of the majority of the people. But when they heard that the Persians were about to cross into Europe, the Thessalians sent messengers to the Isthmus where the conference of the Greek alliance was being held. The Thessalian messengers joined the conference and this is what they said. 'Greeks – the pass of Mount Olympus must be defended to protect Thessaly and all Greece from war. We are ready to do our share, but you must send a large force as well. Otherwise we have to tell you that we will agree terms with the Persians. We are not prepared to die for the rest of Greece on our own in such an exposed position. If you decide not to send help, you cannot make us stay on your side. Nothing can force us to do what we cannot do. We shall just have to find a way of saving ourselves.'

The Greeks decided to send an army to Thessaly by sea to defend the pass. They got a force together and sailed up the Euripus, the channel between Euboea and the mainland. On reaching Alus they disembarked and marched to Thessaly, leaving the ships. They went as far as the pass of Tempe, which runs from Thessaly to the lowlands of Macedonia between the mountains of Olympus and Ossa, following the river Peneus. Here the Greeks took up position. There were about 10,000 hoplites and the Thessalian cavalry in support with Evanetus in command of the Lacedaemonian contingent and Themistocles in command of the Athenian.

The Greeks only stayed at Tempe a few days. A message came from Alexander, the king of Macedon, advising them to with-draw before the invaders overran them. Alexander also told them how large the invading army and fleet were and they decided to take his advice. It seemed sound, and they thought he was on their side. However, I think the Greeks retreated because they were frightened. They found out there was another way into Thessaly through the highlands of Macedonia, the route Xerxes' army, in fact, took. So the Greeks went back to their ships and returned to the Isthmus.

This expedition to Thessaly took place when Xerxes was at Abydos and about to cross over from Asia into Europe. The Thessalians, left without allies, hesitated no longer. They committed themselves whole-heartedly to the Persians and made themselves very useful to the King in the events that followed.

On the Greeks' return to the Isthmus the question of where and how to make a stand and Alexander's message were fully debated. A decision was taken to defend the pass of Thermopylae. This pass had two advantages over the one into Thessaly: it was narrower and it was also nearer home. At the same time a decision was taken to send the fleet up to Artemisium. The two positions were close together and communication between them would be easy.

It would have made good sense to take up a defensive position
further north than Thermopylae but Herodotus says too little
about the expedition for it to be understood in any detail. For
instance, he says nothing about any related defensive moves at
sea. Yet if the Persians had been allowed to land a large force
to the south of the Greek position, or to make straight for
Athens or the Peloponnese, the war would have gone very
differently.

If Xerxes was still at Abydos when the Greeks took up their
position at Tempe, they were under no immediate threat of
attack. Also they would have known about the alternative
inland route through Macedonia into Thessaly. Why, then, did
they leave so quickly, and why did they go there in the first
place? Perhaps the expedition was an attempt to persuade the
northern Greeks to join their alliance in actively resisting the
Persians. If this had been successful, the first line of defence on
land could have been further north than it actually was. The
rest of the Greek fleet would have taken up an appropriate
position in support. Artemisium would have been the most
likely place for this because the coastline running north to
Tempe is rugged and dangerous with no beaches or harbours
of any size on it; it would have been very difficult for the
Persians to land on it any force, especially if the Thessalians
opposed them.

FIRST LINE OF DEFENCE

At Artemisium the sea passes through a narrow channel between
the island of Sciathos and the mainland of Magnesia. Artemisium itself is a bay on the north coast of Euboea at the end of this
channel and a temple of Artemis stands there.

The pass through Trachis into southern Greece is mostly
about fifty yards (50 m) wide but at Thermopylae it is even narrower. At Alpeni to the east and Anthela on the river Phoenix to
the west, it is only wide enough for a single wagon. To the south
and west of the pass there is no way through the steep, high
mountains which run to the peak of Oeta. To the north lies the
sea, full of shallows. There are thermal springs in the pass which
give it its name; the locals call them the Cauldrons. There is also
a shrine to Heracles nearby. There is a wall across this pass and a
long time ago it had gates in it. It was built by the Phocians who

feared an attack from the Thessalians. The wall is very old and most of it had fallen down in the course of time so the Greeks now built it up again to bar the Persians' way into Attica. They intended to get their supplies from the nearby village of Alpeni.

After careful consideration these were the positions the Greeks decided were most suitable. They came to the conclusion that here they would be able to prevent the Persians bringing their great weight of numbers to bear or using their cavalry. Here the Greeks decided to meet the invaders and, when they heard that the Persians had reached Pieria, they left the Isthmus. Some marched to Thermopylae, others sailed for Artemisium, all quickly moving to their positions.

Meanwhile the Delphians, fearing for themselves and for Greece, questioned Apollo about the future through their oracle. The answer they received was:

> Pray to the winds.
> They will be powerful allies.

The Delphians immediately passed the oracle's message on to those Greeks who wanted to fight for their freedom. In their great fear of the Persians, the Greeks were everlastingly thankful for this message.

FIRST BLOOD

Xerxes' fleet left Therma and ten of the fastest ships headed straight for Sciathos. Three Greek ships were on patrol there, one from Aegina, one from Troezene and one from Athens. They sighted the Persian ships and made a dash for safety. The Persians chased them and quickly captured the Troezenian. They picked out the best looking of the hoplites on board, took him up to the bows of the ship and cut his throat, making a sacrifice of the best of the first Greeks they captured. The name of the man offered up in this way was Leon; perhaps his name had something to do with his fate.

The Aeginetan ship gave the Persians some trouble. Pytheas, one of the hoplites, distinguished himself that day. His ship was taken but he went on fighting until he was terribly hacked about. Finding he was still breathing when he fell, the Persians he had fought with did everything they could to keep him alive because of his bravery and dressed his wounds with ointment and linen bandages. Then they took him back to their base and put him on display for the whole army to see. They showed their admiration for him by treating him kindly but they treated everyone else from the ship as slaves.

So two ships were taken while the third ran aground in the mouth of the Peneus. The Persians captured the ship itself, but not its Athenian crew. The moment they had run the ship aground the men jumped ashore and made their way back to Athens through Thessaly on foot. The Greeks positioned at Artemisium were told what had happened by fire signals from Sciathos. The information frightened them and they withdrew to Chalcis, intending to hold the Euripus channel. But they left lookouts on high ground in Euboea.

Three of the ten Persian ships ran aground on the reef called The Ant that lies between Sciathos and Magnesia and the Persians promptly set up a stone marker on the rocks. Then, with their course clearly plotted, the whole fleet set sail from Therma. It was Pammon of Scyros who actually showed them where the reef lay in the channel.

A day's sailing brought the Persian fleet to Sepias in Magnesia and the beach between the town of Casthanea and the headland at Sepias. So far neither the army nor the navy had suffered any loss. By my calculations the numbers were as follows: from Asia there were 1,207 triremes and 3,000 fifty-oared ships with a total of 517,610 men on board; adding on the land forces brought from Asia, the grand total was 2,317,610 not counting non-combatants such as servants and the crews of the supply ships. The forces that Europe supplied must also be added on, though the numbers have to be guessed. The Greeks of Thrace and the islands nearby sent 120 triremes and the following sent soldiers for the land forces: the Thracians, the Paeonians, the Chalcidians, the Pierians, the Macedonians and others, adding by my reckoning another 300,000. Assuming that there was roughly the same number of non-combatants as fighting men, Xerxes, son of Darius, led 5,283,220 men to Cape Sepias and the pass of Thermopylae.

No-one can say with any accuracy how many cooking women, concubines and eunuchs there were, not to mention the transport animals and Indian dogs following behind – there must have been so many! I'm not at all surprised that some of the rivers they came to ran dry but it amazes me that there were enough supplies for so many tens of thousands. Out of all these tens of thousands there was no man more worthy of supreme command, in stature or nobility, than Xerxes.

BOREAS

The Persian fleet reached Magnesia and the beach between Cape Sepias and the town of Casthanea. The ships that arrived first moored close to the shore but the rest had to anchor further out since the beach was not very long; they had to lie eight rows deep with their bows pointing out to sea and this was how they spent the night. But at dawn the clear and calm weather suddenly changed. A heavy sea boiled up and a fierce storm with a gale from the east swept down on them. (This wind is called a Hellesponter by the people who live in the area.) Some of the Persians noticed the wind was getting up and those who were in positions where they could do something about it beached their ships before the storm reached them, so they and their ships survived. But the ships that were caught at sea had no chance of riding out the storm. Some were driven onto the rocks known as the Ovens, some onto the beach. Others were wrecked off Cape Sepias or off Casthanea.

There is a story that the Athenians had prayed to Boreas, the north wind, for help. They had been advised to do this by the Delphic oracle. Seeing that a storm was building up, or even sooner, they sacrificed and called upon Boreas. They prayed that he would come to their aid and destroy the Persian ships just as he had done before at Athos. I cannot say if Boreas made his attack on the Persians because of this, but the Athenians say that he had helped them previously and did act on their behalf on this occasion. Anyway, on their return home they dedicated a temple to the god by the river Ilissus.

According to the lowest estimate at least four hundred warships were wrecked in this disaster, with terrible loss of lives and equipment. The other ships destroyed, such as corn transports, were beyond counting. The generals in command of the fleet feared that the pounding that they had suffered would encourage the Thessalians to turn on them and so they had a high palisade built from the wreckage of the ships. The storm blew for three days and in the end the Magi put a stop to it by sacrificing and chanting spells – or maybe the wind dropped of its own accord.

FIRST ENCOUNTER AT ARTEMISIUM

The lookouts on Euboea ran back from their positions on the heights with news of the wrecking of the Persian fleet. At this, the Greeks prayed to Poseidon their defender and poured offerings of wine, then rowed quickly back to Artemisium. They expected to find only a few ships facing them there. When the wind had dropped and the sea had calmed, the Persians launched their ships and sailed along the coast. They rounded the headland of Magnesia, went into the gulf of Pagasae and put in at Aphetae.

Fifteen Persian ships put to sea a long way behind the rest. They sighted the Greek ships off Artemisium, thought they were their own fleet and sailed straight into the midst of their enemies. Their commander was Sandoces, governor of Cyme in Aeolis. At one time he had been a King's Judge and Darius had ordered that he be crucified for taking bribes. But when he was actually hanging there the King came to the conclusion that Sandoces had done more good to the royal house than harm, decided he had acted with more haste than wisdom, and set him free. So Sandoces escaped death at the hands of King Darius, but when he sailed in amongst the Greeks he was not going to be lucky a second time. The Greeks saw the fifteen Persian ships sailing towards them, realised their mistake, went out to meet them and captured them with ease. After questioning the men and finding out all they wanted to know about Xerxes' forces, they sent them off to the Isthmus in chains.

The Persians and the Greeks were already in contact at sea and on land the first battle ground had been chosen. It was now August, a month in which rough weather is to be expected in the Aegean. The Persians should have sailed down the coast of Thessaly a little earlier. The storm which caught them at Casthanea certainly helped the Greeks, and it helps Herodotus by allowing him to apply some generous arithmetic to match the Persian fleet more evenly to the Greek in the battles that followed.

The small action off Sciathos would certainly not have caused the Greeks to withdraw all the way from Artemisium to Chalcis. Thermopylae could only be held if the coast to the south was protected and the Greek fleet could not have done this from a position so far back. Here Herodotus clearly misunderstood what he was told or was badly misinformed.

5   A fallen king

The battle of Thermopylae concludes Book 7 of the *History*. It took place on the same three days as the fighting off Artemisium which begins Book 8. The battle was glorious and heroic, and also a disaster. Herodotus does full justice to the glory and the heroism in a narrative that has an appropriately epic feel to it; he does not treat the battle as a disaster. The Greeks would not have thought it a disaster at the time because the heroism and glorious death of these few Greeks was an inspiration to their brother Greeks for whom they died. There were also misjudgements (or worse) to be covered up. It is not surprising that here Herodotus leaves key questions unanswered and unasked and mixes so much exaggeration and embroidery with the main facts and the more convincing details. It is in any case, an inspiring story, and its immediate and lasting impact is a historical fact.

King Xerxes and the Persian army had now reached Malis. The Greeks were positioned in the pass at Thermopylae. The Persians had control of all Greece to the north, the Greeks held all that lay to the south.

These were the Greeks waiting for the Persians at Thermopylae: 300 Spartan hoplites, 500 Tegeans, 500 Mantineans, 120 from Orchomenus in Arcadia, 1,000 from the rest of Arcadia, 400 Corinthians, 200 from Phlius and 80 Mycenaeans; from Boeotia there were 700 Thespians and 400 Thebans. In addition the Locrians, in full force, and 1,000 Phocians came when called upon. The Greeks sent for them with the message that they were an advance guard and that the rest of the allies were expected any day. 'With the sea strongly defended by the Athenians and the Aeginetans and the rest of the naval contingent, you have nothing to fear,' they argued. 'It is a man, not a god invading Greece. No mortal man was ever born, or ever will be, without his allotted share of misfortune – the greatest misfortunes fall upon the greatest men. Being a mortal man, the invader will certainly fail.' This persuaded the Locrians and Phocians to march and join the Greeks in Trachis.

Each city's contingent had its own general. The most highly respected, and commander-in-chief of the whole force, was Leonidas of Lacedaemon, one of the Kings of Sparta and a descendant of Heracles. His wife was Cleomenes' daughter. The three hundred Spartans he brought with him were specially selected and all fathers of sons. He also brought along the Thebans mentioned above. They were the only Greeks Leonidas specifically wanted to include in his force. The reason for this was that the Thebans had often been accused of wanting to join up with the Persians. Leonidas therefore called upon them to fight in the war to see whether they would send men or abandon the Greek alliance openly. The Thebans sent men, but they had other plans.

The Spartans sent this advance force under Leonidas to encourage the allies to take the field and not go over to the Persian side; some Greeks already had deserted and others would if they saw the Spartans hanging back. They intended to march fast and in full force later leaving only a garrison in Sparta, but they had to celebrate the feast of the Carneia before they could leave. The rest of the Greeks had similar plans. The Olympic festival fell at this time so they only sent advance contingents. No-one thought a decisive engagement at Thermopylae would come so soon.

This was the planning, then. But when the Persians approached the entrance to the pass, the Greeks at Thermopylae were alarmed and there was talk of retreating. The Peloponnesians wanted to fall back on the Peloponnese and hold the Isthmus but the Phocians and Locrians reacted angrily to this suggestion. Leonidas cast his vote for staying and sent messengers to the allied cities for help since he had too few men to hold off the Persian army.

While this discussion was going on, Xerxes sent a scout on horseback to see how many Greeks there were and what they were doing. While still in Thessaly he had heard that a small force had assembled there, led by the Lacedaemonians with Leonidas of the house of Heracles in command. The horseman rode up to the position and looked it over, but he could not see all of it. The wall which the Greeks were now guarding had been rebuilt and it was not possible to see the men beyond it, but he could see the men in front and their weapons ready beside them. At that moment it was the Lacedaemonians who happened to be positioned in front of the wall. The Persian scout was amazed to see that some were stripped and doing exercises and some were combing their hair. He made a note of their numbers and saw all he wanted without anyone preventing him, then rode back. Nobody took any notice of him or pursued him.

He told Xerxes all he had seen and the King could not make sense of it. He did not know that the Spartans were preparing themselves to kill to the best of their ability and to be killed. He found their behaviour laughable and sent for Damaratus to ask him about it, hoping to find out what it meant.

'I told you about these men before, when we began this expedition,' Damaratus said. 'You laughed when I told you how I saw your plans would turn out. My task is to tell you the truth, King. Now listen. These men have come to fight us for the pass. They are getting ready to do this, following their custom. When they are about to face death, they wash and comb their hair.

'But know this, King. If you defeat these men and those who wait in Sparta, no other nation on earth will stand or lift a hand against you. Now you face the finest and most kingly city, and the best men in Greece.' Xerxes was not persuaded. He waited four days, expecting the Greeks to run away. He thought their unwillingness to retreat was simply reckless folly.

THE BATTLE BEGINS

On the fifth day Xerxes became angry and sent the Medes and Cissians to attack with orders to take the Greeks alive and bring them into his presence. Many Medes fell as they pressed home their attack. Others followed in their place. They were well beaten but would not be driven back. But everyone – and especially the King – could see that though the Medes were many, there were few real men amongst them.

The battle went on all day. The Medes were withdrawn eventually, they had been so badly mauled. Then the picked troop of Persians known as the Immortals, under Hydarnes, went into the attack. It was thought they would have no trouble dealing with the Greeks but when they took them on, they did no better than the Medes. They were fighting with shorter spears than the Greeks and, in the narrow pass, they could not bring their weight of numbers to bear.

The Spartans fought superbly, showing the difference between skilled fighters and unskilled. One of their best tactics was to turn their backs and pretend to run. The Persians would come shouting and clattering after them and, when they were about to catch up, the Spartans turned and faced them and killed an immense number. Only a few Spartans fell. After failing to gain any ground attacking in waves or in any other way, the Persians withdrew. While these attacks were going on it is said that the King leapt up from his throne three times in fear for his army.

SECOND DAY

Next day the Persians were no more successful. They attacked again because they hoped that the Greeks would not be able to stand up to them this time; they were so few and would, the Persians hoped, be weakened by their wounds. But the Greeks stood their ground. Each city's contingent took its turn in the front line, except for the Phocians who were positioned up on the mountain to guard the track there. So the Persians fell back once again; the resistance was as tough as it had been the day before.

The King could see no way of solving the problem that faced him until Epialtes, the Malian, came to see him. Hoping for a large reward, Epialtes told the King about the track that led over the mountain to Thermopylae. Epialtes was the man who brought death to the Greeks who stayed. Here I record his guilt. Xerxes was pleased with Epialtes' offer to act as guide. In good spirits he sent off Hydarnes and his men and they started out from the camp at about the time the lamps are lit.

The Malians who lived in the area discovered this path and had used it to lead the Thessalians against the Phocians at the time when the Phocians had closed the pass with a wall to shelter them from invasion. Ever since, the weakness of the position had been well known to the Malians. The path begins by the river Asopus which flows through the gorge here; both the path and the mountain have the same name – Anopaea. The path runs along a ridge and ends at the town of Alpeni, the Locrian town nearest to Malis; it is narrowest near the rock known as Black Buttocks. Following this path, the Persians crossed the Asopus and marched all night with the mountains of Oeta on their right and the mountains of Trachis on their left.

THIRD DAY

As dawn broke they reached the highest point of the ridge. Here the thousand Phocian hoplites were in position, as I have already mentioned, guarding the path and protecting their own country. The pass below was held as described; the Phocians had volunteered to defend this position.

The Phocians only found out what the Persians were doing when they had almost reached them because the mountain is completely covered with oak trees and they made the climb without being seen. It was a still morning, though, and the leaves lying thick under their feet made a great rustling. Hearing this, the Phocians jumped to their feet and put on their armour but, in a moment, the Persians were there. They were surprised to see men arming and to find themselves facing an army when they had not expected any opposition. Hydarnes, afraid that the Phocians might be Spartans, asked Epialtes who they were. With the question answered, he quickly lined his men up for battle. Showered with arrows the Phocians retreated towards the peak of the mountain. They thought the Persians had come to attack them and prepared themselves to die. But the Persians paid no more attention to them and set off down the mountain, moving fast.

The seer Megistias gave the Greeks at Thermopylae their first warning. He looked at the signs as he sacrificed and predicted death for them that morning. Then, while it was still dark, deserters came with information of the Persian flanking movement, and then, after the dawn, the lookouts came running down from the heights. The Greeks discussed what to do and opinions varied. Some were against leaving the position, others thought differently. The army divided; some contingents left and went home to their own cities, others prepared to stay where they were with Leonidas.

It is said that Leonidas himself sent those contingents away to save their lives, but he did not think it right that he and the Spartans with him should retreat from the position they had come to defend in the first place. Another view, the one I take myself, is this: Leonidas ordered the others to leave when he realised that they were far from enthusiastic as allies and unwilling to share in the danger that they all faced. Retreat was dishonourable as far as he was concerned, however. By staying behind Leonidas won great glory; he also secured the future of Sparta. For the Spartans had gone to Delphi to ask about the war as soon as it began and the Pythia had prophesied that either Sparta would be overthrown or one of her kings would fall. She gave her prophecy in these verses:

Your doom, dwellers in Sparta's wide streets –
Either your mighty, far-famed city will be sacked
Or else all Lacedaemon will lament
A fallen king of the blood of Heracles.
Not the strength of bulls or lions can hold your foe.
He has the strength of Zeus.
Nothing will hold him
Until one or other is destroyed.

Leonidas had this in mind and he wanted the Spartans to have all the glory. So he sent the allies home; I do not think he wanted to have them going off in disorder as the result of a dispute.

One of my main pieces of evidence is this – Megistias the seer, an Acharnanian, the man who foretold the fate in store for the army, was clearly ordered to leave by Leonidas to prevent him dying with the others. But he would not go and made his only son who was serving in the army go in his place.

So the allies whom Leonidas ordered to leave went home and only the Thespians and the Thebans stayed with the Lacedaemonians. The Thebans remained unwillingly, as Leonidas' hostages, in fact. But the Thespians were very willing to stay; they refused to desert Leonidas and his men and stayed to share their death.

The sun rose. Xerxes poured out offerings of wine then waited till about the time that the market place fills before ordering the attack. He was acting on Epialtes' advice that the path down from the mountain ridge was much quicker and more direct than the path climbing round and up it.

So, the barbarians made their attack and the Greeks with Leonidas went out to meet them, knowing they were going forward to their deaths. Up to now they had been fighting in defence of the wall and moving out only to the narrow part of the pass but this time they went much further forward into more open ground. Many barbarians fell. The officers drove their men on with whips from behind, lashing them forward. Many fell into the sea and drowned, many more were trampled to death; it is impossible to describe the slaughter. The Greeks knew that death was closing in on them with the force coming round the mountain so they fought with all their strength and with suicidal fury. By now most of their spears were broken and they were killing Persians with their swords.

At this point in the battle Leonidas fell after fighting heroically. Other famous Spartans fell by his side and I know their names (I know the names of all three hundred). On the Persian side two of Xerxes' brothers fell. The fight to win Leonidas' body was tremendous. Finally, the Greeks' courage was rewarded and they managed to drag it away, beating off the enemy four times in the process.

This was how the battle went till the men with Epialtes arrived, then the character of the fighting changed. The Greeks fell back to the narrowest part of the pass and positioned themselves (all except the Thebans) on a small hill. This is at the entrance to the pass where the stone lion now stands in memory of Leonidas. There the Greeks fought on against the Persians with their swords, those that still had them, and with their bare hands and with their teeth. There the barbarians overwhelmed them with a bombardment of arrows and spears; those attacking from the front destroyed the defensive wall and, with the force that came round the mountain, completely surrounded them.

All the Lacedaemonians and Thespians were heroes, but the bravest of them all is said to have been Dieneces, the Spartan. The story is that before the battle a man from Trachis told him there were so many Persians that their arrows would hide the sun. Dieneces was quite unimpressed. 'Good news,' he said. 'If the Persians hide the sun, we can fight them in the shade.'

All who died at Thermopylae were buried where they fell. The inscription above their grave reads:

> From Pelops' land four thousand
> Stood in battle here
> Against three thousand thousand.

This was for all the fallen. There is an inscription for the Spartans only:

> Friend, tell Lacedaemon
> Here we lie
> Obedient to our orders.

There is also an inscription for Megistias, the seer:

> In memory of Megistias, slain by the Persians:
> He had clear vision of his fate
> But stayed beside his king to die.

The great poet, Simonides, wrote these lines because Megistias was his friend.

The Thebans fought against the King's army with the other Greeks for a while because they were forced to. But when they saw the battle turning the Persians' way, as the Greeks began to fall back towards the hill, they split off. They went up to the Persians with hands outstretched saying they were on their side (which was, indeed, true) and had been amongst the first to give earth and water to the king, and that they had been forced to come to Thermopylae against their will and could not be blamed for the crimes committed against the King.

So the Thebans survived, with the help of the Thessalians who made representations on their behalf. However, they were not completely fortunate because the barbarians killed some of them as they came over to their lines and the rest were branded with the royal mark on Xerxes' orders.

THE REASON WHY

Herodotus says Leonidas was sent to Thermopylae with such a small force because the Greeks were busy with two important religious festivals and because they did not expect a decisive battle so soon. Neither reason seems very convincing. At this time there were 271 Greek triremes at Artemisium, each with a crew of approximately 200 men; ten of these ships were Spartan. So there were in the fleet over 50,000 Greeks missing the Olympics and 2,000 Spartans missing the Carneia, and there can be no doubt that a decisive battle was thought to be imminent at sea.

The Spartans and the rest of the Peloponnesians must have delayed sending a large force for some other reason. Perhaps it was this: they could not be confident that the Greek fleet would survive its first real encounter with the Persians. A defeat at Artemisium would have left their precious hoplites exposed to a more mobile and numerous enemy with command of the sea; and they would be a long way from the Isthmus, their next line of defence if Themistocles' strategy failed. The Persians could have made retreat to the Isthmus very difficult and costly, if not impossible. The danger for a force as small as Leonidas' was even greater but it could provide the fleet with the support it needed on land for long enough, at much less risk to the Peloponnesians' future prospects, if the fleet failed. Leonidas and his men, specially picked so that each left a son behind him, knew all this. It is the true meaning of their epitaph. The prophecy was its justification.

Anopaea

It would not have taken Xerxes long to find there was a way round Leonidas' position. It was local knowledge and he had local help. It is unlikely that he wasted many men or much energy in the frontal attacks which Herodotus describes so graphically while discovering exactly how to use this knowledge. It seems Leonidas misjudged the speed and efficiency with which the Persians would outflank him along the path of Anopaea; he should not have forgotten that they were mountain fighters. The Phocians were certainly taken by surprise. The rustling of dead leaves in the stillness of the dawn must have been very clearly etched in their memories. And they were surprised a second time; the Persians hardly bothered with them. The Phocians' inadequacy at this moment was, perhaps, an example of the 'hoplite mentality' which Mardonius ridiculed, though there is no suggestion that they lacked courage. They were probably too few in any case.

Once the Persians had found the path Leonidas had no option, even if he ever had any. The position was lost and he had to save as much of his force as he could. The Greeks could not afford to lose that many hoplites or to risk the effect of their deaths on the morale and unity, such as it was, of their alliance. He and his Spartans would fight a rear-guard action because honour demanded that they stay and to make sure the job was done properly. The Thespians also volunteered and it is very unlikely the Thebans stayed against their will (it would have been the Thebans who stayed at home who sold out to the Persians).

By the time the last Spartan died, enough time had been bought. The rest of Leonidas' force was out of the Persians' reach. On the sea the damage done to the Persian fleet, by the weather and the Greeks, was sufficient to have decisive consequences. Even if Leonidas had been able to hold out longer, securing the coast to the south and Euboea at their backs, the Greeks would have had to retreat to Salamis, the nearest secure and substantial docks. There they could repair the damage they had suffered, replace their casualties and prepare to meet the Persian fleet once more.

THE NEXT MOVE

After the battle Xerxes sent for Damaratus to ask him a question. 'Damaratus, you are a good man,' he began. 'I am persuaded of this by your truthfulness, for everything has turned out as you said it would. Now answer me this – how many Lacedaemonians are left, and how many are fighters like these, or are they all as good?'

Damaratus replied, 'King, there are many men in Lacedaemon and many cities. But, I'll answer your exact question. There is a city in Lacedaemon called Sparta and there are about 8,000 men in that city. All are equal to the men who fought here. The rest of the Lacedaemonians are not their equals; but they are still good men.'

'How shall we defeat these people most easily?' said the King. 'Come, tell me, Damaratus. You have been their king and understand their thinking.'

'King, this is the best way to go about it,' Damaratus answered. 'Send three hundred ships to Lacedaemon. There is an island off the coast called Cythera which they should use as their base. That will alarm the Lacedaemonians. With war close to home they will not go to the help of the rest of Greece.'

Achaemenes spoke next. He was one of Xerxes' brothers and commander of the fleet. He heard this conversation and was worried that Xerxes might do what Damaratus advised. 'King,' he said, 'I see you are taking advice from a man who envies your success and who might even betray you. This is the way with the Greeks; they are jealous of success and despise power greater than their own. Four hundred of your ships have already been wrecked. If you detach another three hundred to sail round the Peloponnese, the enemy will be able to face you in battle; they will not be able to if you keep the fleet together. Also, the fleet and the land army, advancing side by side, will be able to support each other.'

'I think you are right, Achaemenes,' said Xerxes. 'But Damaratus has given me the advice he thinks best. I will not accept any suggestion that he does not have my best interests at heart. Therefore I order you to put an end to this slander; Damaratus is my guest and my friend.'

Xerxes then went over to look at the bodies. His men told him that Leonidas was the Lacedaemonians' king and general and he ordered them to cut off his head and impale it on a stake. Of all the pieces of evidence, this is the most significant, I think, that Xerxes was terribly angered by Leonidas. He would never otherwise have treated his body so sacrilegiously; I know this because the Persians customarily treat brave men with exceptional respect and honour.

6   The foundation-stone of freedom

ARTEMISIUM

Book 8 of the *History* begins with the fighting in the straits
between Artemisium and Aphetae which took place on the
same three days as the fighting at Thermopylae. At
Artemisium the Greek alliance was fully committed: defeat at
Artemisium would effectively have ended the war because then
the Persians would have had command of the sea.

Artemisium was a well-chosen position. The Greeks had a
good bay in which to beach their ships and camp with the
security of Euboea at their backs. The island would remain
secure as long as they closed the Euripus channel and covered
the northeast coastline, and as long as Leonidas' force kept the
Persian army from advancing further south to points where
crossings could easily be made. If the Greeks used the right
tactics there would not be room for the Persians to make the
best of their superior numbers, manoeuvrability and
seamanship. Also, as long as withdrawal was still possible, the
Greeks had friendly harbours, docking facilities and
reinforcements to fall back on. The Persians, on the other
hand, had an inhospitable coastline behind them to the north
and only the resources they could carry with them.

Eurybiades, a Spartan, was commander-in-chief of the
Greeks, but Themistocles, leading the Athenian fleet, would
have been most influential in all the planning. The Athenian
fleet was essential to a co-ordinated Greek resistance and,
within reason, the rest of the allies had to do what
Themistocles and Athens wanted them to do. It is very
unlikely that he expected to stop the Persians at Artemisium or
do more than weaken them for the next and decisive
encounter, for which he already had the straits of Salamis in
mind. Also, he probably wanted an opportunity for the Greek
fleet and the Athenians, in particular, to gain some much-
needed battle experience, with the chance of putting it to use
later on.

Triremes
The two fleets facing each other across the straits consisted
mainly of triremes. The trireme was a type of warship adopted
by the Greeks only shortly before the Persian War. It was
developed by the Phoenicians and other sea powers of the
eastern Mediterranean. The Greek triremes were slower and
less manoeuvrable than those in the Persian fleet, and the
Phoenicians, at least, were better seamen than the Greeks.

A trireme was approximately a hundred feet (30m) long and
twelve feet (4m) wide. It had a mast and a sail but these were
not used in battle normally (except to run away) and were
probably only effective in a following wind. The ship was
driven by oars, 75 to a side in the early fifth century, with the
oarsmen working their oars from three tiers of benches. A top
speed of about six knots could be sustained for a short burst.

The trireme's main weapon was its ram, a solid, bronze-clad
timber protruding from the bows at water level. The ship also
carried a squad of twenty or thirty fighting men armed as they
would be for a battle on land. Their function was to board an
enemy ship after a ramming, when the two ships were locked
together, and to repel boarders. The oarsmen and small crew
of sailors were unarmed and defenceless.

In the Greek fleet the rowers were free citizens doing their
military service. Normally they were drawn from those who
could not serve as hoplites because they were not rich enough
to buy the weapons and armour. But they would have shared
in the decisions that brought the battle about and in the
decisions that had given them their part to play in it.
Moreover, they were defending their homes and families, and
the democratic freedoms they believed in. This must have been
some compensation for any lack of skill or experience,
numerical disadvantage or inferiority in their ships. The
oarsmen in the fleets that made up the Persian navy may not
have been slaves, but they were not serving the Persian empire
by choice and lacked the motivation of their Greek opponents.

Triremes could only carry a limited amount of food and
water for their crews. They were not designed for long
passages or to withstand rough weather. It was usual to beach
them at night as it would have been impossible for 200 men to
sleep on board except in relays and probably in great
discomfort. For these reasons the two opposing fleets needed
secure coasts or islands within easy reach if they were to
operate effectively. This is why both invasion and defence were
combined operations on land and sea in 480. And this is why
the story of the bribing of the Greek generals can be

discounted as one of a number invented to discredit
Themistocles, although it truly reflects the tensions within the
Greek high command.

The Greek fleet at Artemisium consisted of the following: 127
ships from Athens (the Plataeans, who were no sailors, helped
man some of these out of courage and their devotion to the Greek
cause); 40 ships from Corinth; 20 ships from Megara; 20 more
ships from Athens but manned by Chalcidians; 18 ships from
Aegina; 12 from Sicyon; 10 from Lacedaemon; 8 from Epidaurus;
7 from Eretria; 5 from Troezene; 2 from Styra. There were 271
triremes altogether. Styra also sent two fifty-oared ships and
Opuntian Locris sent seven.

The supreme commander was a Spartan, Eurybiades, because
the other allies said they would split up the fleet rather than allow
an Athenian to lead them. At an earlier stage it had been suggested that the Athenians should command the Greek navy but
there was resistance to this and the Athenians gave way. They
considered that the survival of Greece was the greatest priority
and reckoned that a dispute over who should lead would be fatal.
They were right about this; 'strife within the family' in war is as
far removed from unity as war from peace. Understanding this
well, the Athenians did not press their claim; at least they gave
way to the others as long as they had real need of them. For when
the Persians had been driven back and the fight was for Persian
territory, the Athenians took over command from the Spartans.
They gave Pausanias' high-handed behaviour as their reason for
this ... But that is something that happened later on.

The fleet the Greeks saw facing them at Artemisium was in a
far better state and far larger than they had expected. They were
alarmed and began to plan retreat. Realising this, the Euboeans
begged Eurybiades to stay and give them a little time to move
their children and households to safety. They could not persuade
Eurybiades but they did manage to bribe the Athenian general,
Themistocles, with thirty talents to ensure that the Greek fleet
stayed where it was and fought off the coast of Euboea. Themistocles managed this by giving Eurybiades five talents out of this
sum as though it was a personal gift. Only one other general, Adimantus the Corinthian, was unwilling to follow Eurybiades'
lead; Themistocles sent him three talents and he too was won
over. So the Euboeans got what they wanted and Themistocles

gained from the deal as well, secretly keeping the rest of the money.

The Persians had reached Aphetae early in the afternoon of that day. They had already heard that the Greek fleet at Artemisium was small and, when they saw it, they were eager to attack and capture it. However, they decided not to attack the Greeks there and then because they thought that the Greeks would try to escape when they saw them advancing and get away under cover of darkness. The Persians did not want a single Greek to escape. Therefore they sent a squadron of two hundred ships round Euboea to the Euripus on a course that took them the far side of Sciathos to keep them out of sight of the enemy. Their purpose was to bar the Greeks' retreat while the rest of the fleet attacked from the front. No attack was planned for that day or until the signal came that the encircling movement had been completed.

There was a man called Scyllias from Scione with the Persian fleet. He was a very good diver and had salvaged a lot of valuable property for the Persians after their ships had been wrecked at Cape Sepias (he had also acquired a good deal of valuable property for himself at the same time). Scyllias had for some while been planning to desert, but this was the first opportunity he had to do it. I cannot say for sure how he managed to reach the Greeks, but the story that is told is amazing, if it is true. Scyllias is said to have dived into the sea at Aphetae and not come up until he reached Artemisium, swimming about ten miles (16 km) underwater. Now there are a good many stories about this man and some of them have a ring of truth. In this case, it is my view that he got to Artemisium by boat. Anyway he arrived there and told the generals about the ships that had been wrecked and about the squadron sailing round Euboea.

THE BATTLE BEGINS

The Greeks discussed this information and there was a lot of argument. The decision was to stay in a defensive position for that day and then put to sea around midnight and move against the ships coming round Euboea. But no attack came and after waiting till late afternoon the Greeks moved out to attack the barbarians. They wanted to test their strength and tactics.

Xerxes' men, generals and all other ranks alike, thought the Greeks were mad to attack with such a small force. They put to sea confident of an easy victory and they had reason to be confident since their fleet was so much larger and more seaworthy. The Ionians who were fighting on the Persian side unwillingly, and who really supported the Greeks, were very distressed to see the Greeks being surrounded; they thought none of them would ever see his home again. But the Ionians who were fighting willingly on the Persian side competed with each other to be the first to capture an Athenian ship and so win a reward from the King, for the Athenians had been the main topic of conversation in the Persian camp.

On the Greek side a signal was given and the ships formed a circle, bows towards the enemy and sterns towards the centre. At a second signal they set to work and captured thirty barbarian ships although they were tightly hemmed in and prow to prow with the enemy. Night fell and brought the engagement to an inconclusive end and the Greeks sailed back to Artemisium, the barbarians to Aphetae. The barbarians had done less well than they had expected. In the course of the battle only one of the Greeks on the King's side deserted and he was rewarded by the Athenians after the war.

It rained heavily and thundered during the night. The corpses and wreckage from the battle were driven to Aphetae by the storm; they washed up against the prows of the Persian ships and became entangled with their oars. This and the noise of the storm alarmed the Persians greatly and made them think their end had come. They had recovered from the storm off Pelion and the damage it had done only to face a hard battle, and now the rain was pouring down with thunder and lightning, and swollen streams were rushing into the sea. That night was much worse for the ships sailing round Euboea, however. The same storm hit them in the open sea and it *was* the end for them. The wind and rain caught them off the part of the coast of Euboea called the Hollows and drove them headlong onto the rocks there. This was brought about by Zeus himself in order that the Greek and Persian forces should be more evenly matched.

SECOND DAY

The barbarians at Aphetae were glad to see the dawn but, after the sufferings of the night, they made no move all day. However, the Greeks were greatly encouraged by the arrival of 53 more

Athenian ships and the good news of the total destruction of the barbarian force off Euboea. They waited till the same hour as the day before, then sailed out and attacked some Cilician ships, sank them and sailed back to Artemisium as night fell.

THIRD DAY

On the third day, angered by the damage done to them by so few ships and fearing Xerxes' anger, the Persian generals did not wait for the Greeks to make the first move but ordered their fleet to sail out around midday. As it happens, these sea battles took place on the same three days as the land battles at Thermopylae. The objectives for the Greek fleet and the army with Leonidas were the same: to bar the way into Greece. The barbarians' objective was to destroy the Greeks and win entry.

The barbarians sailed towards the Greeks in a crescent formation intending to encircle them. The Greeks held their position, then moved forward and the battle began. The sides were more or less equally matched since Xerxes' fleet was hampered by its own weight of numbers. However, although there were collisions and confusion, the barbarians held their own without yielding, for shame at the prospect of being put to flight by so few. The Greeks lost many ships and men, but the barbarians lost even more. In Xerxes' fleet the Egyptians fought best while the Athenians were the best of the Greeks.

In the end both sides were glad to break off and sail back to their anchorages. But the Greeks took possession of the wreckage and the dead. However, they had taken a terrible battering and the Athenians had suffered worst of all with half their ships damaged. A withdrawal to the south was generally favoured.

Themistocles called the generals together and asked them to order their men to light fires and slaughter the Euboean sheep that had been driven down to the shore, for it was better that they should eat them than the enemy. He said he had a plan that might deprive the King of his best allies and that he, Themistocles, would choose the right moment for their withdrawal to bring them safely home. The generals agreed to all this.

The Greeks had posted two scout ships, one at Trachis to bring word of Leonidas' army to the fleet at Artemisium and one at Artemisium to keep Leonidas informed about the fleet. At this moment the ship from Trachis arrived and told the Greeks about the fate of Leonidas and his army. Without delay, an orderly retreat began and each contingent moved off in turn, the Corinthians going first and the Athenians bringing up the rear.

Themistocles picked the most seaworthy of the Athenian ships and sailed down the coast, calling at all the beaches where there was drinking water. At each one he had a message carved into the rocks for the Ionians with Xerxes' fleet to read. It urged them to come over to the Greek side and to persuade the Carians to desert as well, or, if they were prevented from deserting, to fight half-heartedly. 'Remember, you are descended from us,' the message said, 'and this war was begun by you and not by us.'

The Persians sailed across to Artemisium the next day, then took the city of Histiaea and occupied the northern part of Euboea. At Thermopylae Xerxes had all but a thousand of the twenty thousand Persians who had died, buried in mass graves and hidden under earth and leaves. Then he sent a herald over to the fleet at Histiaea to summon all who wanted to come and see the battlefield. There was a scramble for the boats, because so many wanted to go. When they saw the battlefield they thought all the dead Greeks were Spartans and Thespians although they were also looking at helots, the Spartans' slaves. But they were not deceived by Xerxes' laughable effort to hide the Persian dead from them.

At about this time a few Greek deserters came into the Persian camp. They were asked through an interpreter what the Greeks were doing. The deserters said that the Greeks were celebrating the Olympic festival with athletic contests and horse races. When asked what prize the winners received they told the Persians about the wreath of olive leaves. Hearing this Tigranes, the son of Artabanus, made a most excellent remark although Xerxes called him a coward for it. 'What kind of men have you led us against, Mardonius?' he exclaimed. 'They compete for no reward except honour.'

The Persian army moved south. First it overran Phocis with particularly enthusiastic assistance from the Thessalians, old enemies of the Phocians. Cities and temples were plundered and burned and the Phocians that could escape took to the mountains or found safety in Locris. The army then entered Boeotia, which had gone over to the Persian side, and marched towards Athens. According to Herodotus a force was sent to Delphi to plunder the temples but was driven off by divine intervention – thunderbolts, falling rocks, unearthly shouts and giant hoplites.

The real explanation must be that the Persians decided to spare Delphi. An attack on Delphi would have outraged the Greeks and strengthened their resistance. After the fall of Greece, Delphi might have served the Persians very usefully. There may even have been an understanding between the Persians and some Delphians. In any case, a supernatural explanation for their deliverance would have saved the Delphians potential embarrassment.

The battle of Thermopylae was an important part of the overall strategy but the success at Artemisium was of more practical importance. Because of their losses in battle and the bad weather (though the effect of the latter may be exaggerated), the Persians could not divide their own fleet to attack the Peloponnese and contain the enemy fleet simultaneously. Their newly and painfully acquired respect for Greek sea-power would also have discouraged them from trying this. The poet Pindar, writing not long afterwards, praised Artemisium as the place where 'the sons of Greece laid the shining foundation-stone of freedom'. This was not extravagant praise.

7   Blessed island

Earlier in the year, the decision had been taken to evacuate
Athens and concentrate the Athenian army and fleet on the
island of Salamis, if it proved necessary. The Delphic oracle
may have mentioned Salamis in the 'wooden wall' answer
because the Athenians had specifically asked for advice on this
part of their defensive plan which had been devised by
Themistocles. It was a plan that served the interests of Athens
best but also served the interests of Greece as a whole. Its
development had begun with the ship-building programme
initiated by Themistocles a few years before. Now his powers
of persuasion and skill at presenting strategic arguments were
to be called upon yet again and were probably needed even to
get the rest of the Greek fleet to join the Athenians at Salamis
in the first place.

Herodotus' account of this tense period of waiting and
arguing, which was probably longer than he implies, is
dramatic and, in many aspects, convincing. First it seems
certain that the Peloponnesians will retreat to their home
waters. Attention is then switched to the brave but hopeless
defence of the Acropolis and its efficient capture. Then
Themistocles takes the centre of the stage again and persuades
the Peloponnesians to remain and fight. The scene shifts to the
Persians' camp and there is a suggestion that Xerxes might
undo all Themistocles' work by attacking the Peloponnese on
land without attacking the Greek fleet. Finally, with the
Peloponnesians wavering once more, Themistocles tricks
Xerxes and then joins with his greatest political rival,
Aristides, in a last attempt to convince his allies. This fails but
then a message comes to confirm that retreat is no longer
possible.

SALAMIS

From Artemisium the Greek fleet sailed to the island of Salamis.
The Athenians had asked the fleet to come there so that they
could evacuate their women and children from Attica and so that

they could all discuss what to do next. They called for a conference because they had expected to find the Peloponnesians in full force facing the barbarians in Boeotia but far from what they expected, they had discovered that the Peloponnesians were fortifying the Isthmus. They clearly had decided that the defence of the Peloponnese was the most important thing and that the rest of Greece could be abandoned.

On arriving back at Athens the Athenian generals gave instructions that everyone should make arrangements to move his family and household slaves to safety. Most were sent to Troezene, in the Peloponnese, but some went to Aegina or Salamis. The Athenians were acting fast to obey the oracle, and there was another pressing reason: the Athenians say that a great snake is guardian of the Acropolis and lies in the temple there, and they make it monthly offerings of honey-cake. The honey-cake had always been eaten up, but that month it was not touched. The priestess told the Athenians this and they were all the more eager to evacuate the city if the goddess had abandoned the Acropolis.

The rest of the Greek fleet joined the other ships at Salamis and the whole fleet was much larger than the one that had fought at Artemisium. Eurybiades, the Spartan, was in command but Athens contributed by far the most ships and also the most seaworthy ones. Sparta had 16 ships there and Corinth 40, so, with smaller contributions from other cities, a total of 89 ships came from the Peloponnese. From outside the Peloponnese, in addition to the Athenian fleet of 180, nearly half the total, there were the 20 ships from Megara and 30 from Aegina; the rest of Aegina's fleet was guarding the island but the best ships were sent to fight at Salamis. 20 ships came from Chalcis and smaller numbers from other cities and the few islands that had not surrendered to the Persians. The total was 378 triremes and there were also a few smaller ships.

When all the generals of the Greek alliance had gathered at Salamis, they held a meeting. Eurybiades opened the debate by asking for suggestions as to the most suitable place for a sea-battle. He was against fighting near Athens and favoured choosing somewhere off that part of the Greek mainland still controlled by the alliance. Most of the generals were in favour of sailing to the Isthmus and fighting a sea-battle in defence of the Peloponnese there. They argued that they would find themselves blockaded on an island without any hope of rescue if they lost the battle at Salamis; if they were defeated off the Isthmus, however, they would be able to escape to their own cities.

While the generals from the Peloponnese were putting forward this argument a message arrived that the barbarians had entered Attica and were burning everything in their path. They had already burned the cities of Plataea and Thespia acting on information from the Thebans that neither would come over to their side. It had taken the Persians three months to march from the Hellespont to Athens.

THE FALL OF ATHENS

Athens was deserted but there were some Athenians on the Acropolis, a few temple wardens and poor men who had barricaded themselves in with timbers and planks. They could not afford to make the crossing to Salamis and, besides, they thought they knew the true meaning of the Delphic prophecy about the 'wooden wall'. The Persians took up a position opposite the Acropolis on the hill the Athenians call the Areopagus and shot fire-arrows at the barricade. But the Athenians held out although they were in deadly danger and had been betrayed by their wooden wall. Pisistratids were sent to the Athenians with terms for a truce but they would not listen. Instead, they continued defending themselves; one effective tactic was rolling boulders down on the barbarians as they charged the gates. In fact, for a long time, Xerxes had no idea how to take the position. Eventually, however, the barbarians found a solution to their problem – the prophecy that the whole mainland of Attica would fall under the Persians had to be fulfilled.

At the front of the Acropolis, but to the rear of the gates and the ramp that leads up to them, there is a place that nobody was guarding because nobody thought anyone could climb up to it. Here some Persians scaled the sheer cliff. When the Athenians saw them some flung themselves to their death from the ramparts while others fled to the inner chamber of the temple. The Persians charged the gates, broke them down and slaughtered the Athenians seeking sanctuary inside. Then they plundered the temple and burned down all the buildings on the Acropolis.

Xerxes was now master of Athens and sent off a horseman to Susa to tell Artabanus the good news of his triumph. Next day he ordered the Athenian exiles who were with him to go up on the Acropolis and sacrifice according to their custom – maybe he was instructed to do this by a dream, or perhaps he regretted burning down the temple. Anyway, there is an olive tree sacred to Athene on the Acropolis; this tree was burned by the barbarians in the fire that burned the temple but, on the day after the fire, the Athenians who went to sacrifice saw a new shoot about eighteen inches (50 cm) long sprouting from the charred stump.

THEMISTOCLES' STRATEGY

This section begins with another, rather weak anecdote against Themistocles; it suggests that his defensive plan and the arguments with which he backed it up were someone else's idea. Like all the other speeches in the *History*, Themistocles' speeches are reconstructions with some factual basis. Herodotus' sources would certainly have been able to remember the main arguments even if they had not been present at the various conferences. Here it is more likely that some of the actual words might have been preserved than in most other cases. The debate was, after all, crucial as far as the future of Athens was concerned and Themistocles and his supporters would not have kept the details of it from the rest of the Athenians. Themistocles' closing threat to transplant Athens to Italy would not have been an idle one; it was a possible final course of action which must have been often discussed.

Themistocles returned to his ship after the generals' conference. A certain Athenian asked him what had been decided. On being told that the plan was to sail to the Isthmus and fight there, this Athenian said, 'If the fleet leaves Salamis the Greeks won't be fighting for one country any longer. They will all go home to their cities and it will be impossible even for Eurybiades to keep them together. The allied army will be scattered and Greece will be lost through this stupidity. If you possibly can, try to reverse the decision; try to persuade Eurybiades to change his mind and stay here.'

Themistocles went to Eurybiades' ship and told him all that the Athenian had told him as if it was his own idea, and he added many arguments of his own as well. He persuaded Eurybiades, who came out of his ship and called the generals back to the meeting place. Before Eurybiades could tell the generals what he had called them together for, Themistocles launched into a long and passionate speech. In the middle of it Adimantus, the Corinthian general, said, 'At the Games runners who make a false start get a beating, Themistocles.'

Themistocles answered him mildly, 'But runners who are left on the starting line don't win.' Then he turned to Eurybiades and carried on with his speech. He could not repeat the argument that the allied army would break up if the fleet left Salamis. It would have been quite out of order to make this accusation to the allies' faces, so he used a different line of argument.

'You can save Greece,' he said, 'if you follow my advice and stay here and fight. Do not listen to the others who suggest withdrawing to the Isthmus. Listen and compare the two plans.

'If you take on the enemy at the Isthmus you will be fighting in open water; this would not be to our advantage at all since our fleet is smaller and our ships are slower. In any case you would lose Salamis, Megara and Aegina even if we won the battle, and you would be endangering the whole of Greece by drawing the Persian land army, which would follow the fleet, towards the Peloponnese. But, if you do what I suggest, you will gain these advantages: first, we will win a great victory if we engage their large force with our small fleet in this narrow channel, and the battle goes as is to be expected. Secondly Salamis will be saved, and our women and children too. Thirdly, and this is particularly important from your point of view, you will be defending the Peloponnese just as well in this position. If you take my advice you will keep the enemy away from the Isthmus. If we win, and I predict we shall, the enemy will advance no further but retreat in disorder. We shall have saved Megara, Aegina and Salamis – the island of our prophesied victory. Rational planning brings success, but Zeus gives no assistance to men who make irrational plans.'

Adimantus, the Corinthian, interrupted Themistocles' speech a second time. He said a man without a country had no right to speak and urged Eurybiades not to take a vote on what he proposed; Themistocles should find a country for himself before making any proposals in the council. Then Themistocles spoke most harshly about Adimantus and the Corinthians. Moreover, he made it quite clear that the Athenians with 200 ships fully manned had a greater city and more territory than the Corinthians, and power no Greek city could resist.

Themistocles then turned back to Eurybiades and said, 'Do what is best and stay here; or go, and destroy Greece. Our fleet is vital in this war. If you won't do what I advise we will sail with our families to Siris in Italy; Siris has belonged to Athens for many years and we have been instructed by oracles to colonise the place. You will be lost without your Athenian allies and then you will remember what I told you.' Themistocles' speech made Eurybiades change his mind and so the Greeks at Salamis prepared for battle.

XERXES DECIDES

The Persian invasion force would have picked up new recruits as it advanced, but the lost ships (however many actually were lost) would not have been replaced. Xerxes could not now risk detaching a fleet of any size to threaten the Peloponnese because the rest of the fleet might not be able to contain the Greeks. However, if he had sent the whole fleet against the Peloponnese the Greeks might have been drawn out into the open sea where the Persians would have been at an advantage. But Salamis was an important strategic prize and the autumn was coming soon, which would put an end to naval operations. Xerxes' options were limited, whatever Queen Artemisia may have thought.

The Persian land and sea forces that arrived at Athens and Phaleron were as large as when they had come to Thermopylae and Sepias. The men lost in the great storm and at the battles of Thermopylae and Artemisium had been replaced by new recruits, Melians, Dorians, Locrians and Boeotians, for example, and men from many of the islands. The further the Persians advanced into Greece, the more their ranks were swelled.

Xerxes called together all the commanders of his fleet and sent Mardonius amongst them to test each one by asking the question whether or not the King should fight now. All said he should fight except for Artemisia, Queen of Halicarnassus. She said, 'Tell the King this from me, Mardonius – and I speak as one who has already played a distinguished part in the fighting off Euboea. Tell him to save his ships; tell him not to fight now. Fighting at sea, the Greeks compare with us as men compare in strength to women. Why risk everything in a sea-battle? Athens, the whole reason for the expedition, has been won, and with it the rest of Greece.

'I have this to say to Xerxes: King, if you delay fighting a sea-battle and keep your fleet on the coast here or perhaps even sail for the Peloponnese, you will easily achieve the goal you have set yourself. The Greeks cannot hold together against you for long; you will scatter them and they will go home to their own cities. They have no supplies on Salamis, so I am informed, and it is unlikely that the Peloponnesians will want to fight a sea-battle for Athens if you threaten the Peloponnese with your army. But if you rush into a sea-battle now, I very much fear your fleet will suffer harm and this in turn will have a damaging effect on your army.'

Her friends were afraid that the King would punish Artemisia for advising him so forcibly not to fight. But Xerxes was delighted by the way she had expressed her opinion. He had always thought a great deal of her and now he thought even more highly. All the same, he gave orders for battle. He thought that his men had fought badly off Euboea because he had not been there, but this time he meant to watch them in action. It was too late to fight that day, however, so the Persians prepared for battle the next morning.

THEMISTOCLES CHOOSES HIS MOMENT

If the Persians were going to fight, Themistocles knew that the battle must be fought where and when he chose, and soon. The trick he decided to play may seem incredible but his message was exactly the sort of breakthrough Xerxes was hoping for. He would have been well aware of the uneasy unity of the Greek alliance. He had Greeks in his army and navy, so spying would have been relatively easy, and it was a fact that there was much talk of retreat on Salamis. The Persians had won great victories in the past (the battle of Lade, for example) by exploiting divisions amongst their enemies. Themistocles' trick was a masterpiece of 'doublecross' intelligence.

The Greeks were very frightened, especially the Peloponnesians. The prospect of fighting a sea-battle to protect Athenian territory alarmed them; they feared that if they were defeated they would find themselves blockaded on the island and unable to defend their homes. That same night, in fact, the barbarian army was marching for the Peloponnese.

The Peloponnesians had done all they could to keep the barbarians off their territory. As soon as they heard about the fate of Leonidas' force at Thermopylae they had assembled at the Isthmus under the command of Cleombrotus, Leonidas' brother. They discussed what defensive measures they should take and decided to build a wall across the Isthmus. They used rocks, bricks, timber and baskets of sand and, with thousands of men there, all doing their share and working day and night, they soon completed it.

The Peloponnesians who went to the Isthmus were united by their fear for Greece, but there were others who did not care. A substantial number of cities took no part in the war and, to put it frankly, that was as good as siding with the Persians.

The Peloponnesians at Salamis knew about these defensive preparations but feared for the Peloponnese. At first the men just talked quietly amongst themselves, surprised by Eurybiades' lack of judgement, but at length their uneasiness came out into the open. There was another debate with the same lengthy arguments as before for retreating to the Peloponnese.

Themistocles quietly left the conference when he saw that the voting was going against him and sent a man in a boat to the Persian camp with a message to deliver. The man's name was Sicinnus, one of Themistocles' slaves and tutor to his children, and Themistocles later made him a citizen of Thespia and a rich man. Sicinnus arrived in his boat and said this to the barbarian generals: 'The Athenian general sent me to you secretly, and the other Greek generals know nothing about it. He is the King's friend and wishes for a Persian victory. I am to tell you that the Greeks are demoralised and planning to retreat. You will win your greatest triumph ever, simply by preventing their escape. The Greeks are quarrelling amongst themselves and they won't be able to resist you. You will see them fighting each other, the Greeks who support you against the Greeks who are your enemies.'

Sicinnus delivered this message then quickly took himself off; and the Persians believed it. First they landed a large force on the island of Psyttalea midway between Salamis and the mainland. Then, around midnight, they moved up one wing of the fleet to encircle Salamis and positioned the rest of the fleet to close up the channel as far as Munychia. In this way they planned to trap the Greeks at Salamis and punish them for their resistance at Artemisium. They placed the force on Psyttalea because the battle was likely to be fought all round the island and men would be washed up on it; its task was to assist any friends and kill any of the enemy who came ashore there. The Persians made these moves in silence so that the Greeks should know nothing about them; they had no rest that night.

The Greek generals were still locked in argument. They thought the Persians were in the positions they had last seen them in and did not yet know they were surrounded. But then Aristides, the Athenian, arrived from Aegina. (The Athenians had ostracised him but, from all I have been able to learn, he was the best and most just of them all.) He called Themistocles out of the council. Themistocles was his great rival but he was willing to forget this in view of the danger they were all in. He said to him, 'Themistocles, we must compete now as we have always done. But this time let's see which of us can do the most good for our country. I can tell you that it makes no odds what the Peloponnesians say about sailing away from here; I have seen with my own eyes that they can't do it, even if the Corinthians and Eurybiades himself decide that they should. We are surrounded. Go in there and tell them.'

'Good news and excellent advice,' said Themistocles. 'You have arrived as a witness that what I wanted to happen is happening; in fact this move of the Persians is my doing. The Greeks did not want to fight so it was necessary to force them to. But you brought the good news, so you announce it to them. If I tell them they will think I am making it up; they won't believe me. You tell them and it will be excellent if they believe you. But if they don't, it will make no difference. They can't run away now if we are completely surrounded, as you say we are.'

So Aristides told them, but the argument began all over again. Most of the generals would not believe him. Then a trireme from Tenos arrived, a deserter from the Persian fleet, and the crew assured the Greeks that what Aristides had said was true. Finally, the generals believed what they had been told and the Greeks prepared for battle.

Aristides' appearance on the eve of the battle of Salamis adds to the drama. He was an example of the virtues and political attitudes which Themistocles was considered by his enemies to lack. Aristides had been sent into exile a few years before by the strange process of ostracism. This enabled the Athenians to put an end to power struggles between leading citizens by voting one or other of them into exile for a ten-year period.

Ostracism was supposed to prevent power becoming too concentrated in the hands of individuals but it tended to have exactly the opposite effect: the loser in the voting, who went into exile, often represented the main opposition to the winner and his removal, therefore, increased the winner's power.

Aristides and Themistocles had been rivals for power and the people had chosen that Aristides rather than Themistocles should be exiled, which would have been remembered or known by many of Herodotus' Athenian readers. One of the Athenian emergency measures was to recall the victims of ostracism because it was felt that the city could not afford to be without their services; Aristides would in fact have been able to return earlier in the year.

8   A wooden wall

It would have been very hard for anyone to write a complete
account of the battle of Salamis even immediately afterwards.
The action was spread out over twelve square miles (20 square
km) of water and must have lasted for several hours. There
were several hundred triremes involved and, once the first
phase of the battle was over, the fighting was between
individual ships or small groups. It was impossible to know
what was happening generally; communication was only
possible between ships at very close quarters. Herodotus
collected his information thirty or forty years after the battle: it
is not surprising, therefore, that his account is rather sparse.
However, it is possible to see a pattern and to visualise the
main sequence of events, though Herodotus' account can, of
course, be interpreted in a number of different ways.

The Persians wanted a decisive battle at Salamis. If they
could defeat and destroy the Greek fleet their chances of
overall victory before the end of the campaigning season were
excellent. They reacted to Themistocles' message as they did
because they had to keep the Greek fleet where it was and
prevent any elements of it escaping to become a threat and an
obstacle later in the year or in the following spring.

They could not risk sailing into the narrow part of the
straits in any force in the dark but, if the Greeks did not come
out to meet them, they were committed to attacking at
daybreak. If the Greeks were planning to break out, the
Persian fleet could not return to the beaches of Phaleron for
food and rest. But it could not remain at sea indefinitely
blockading the exits to the straits. The Persians knew as well
as Themistocles did that a battle inside the straits would even
out the odds against the Greeks. But they believed that only
some of the Greeks would resist and that the rest would either
take no part in the fighting or try to escape. The Persians were
confident that they could handle any partial or unco-ordinated
resistance. Any escapers would be met by ships positioned on
either side of the island of Psyttalea and in the narrower
channel to the west of Salamis. The Persians were doing
exactly what Themistocles wanted them to do.

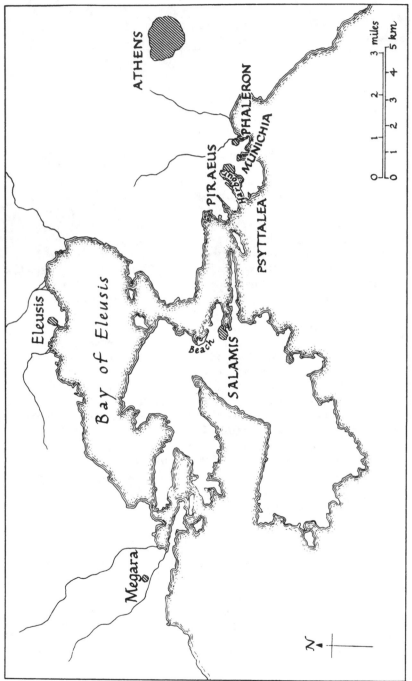

3 Salamis

THE BATTLE OF SALAMIS

Dawn was breaking and the men who were to fight on the ships were called together. Themistocles made the best of all the speeches. In it he compared everything that is good in man's nature and the human condition with everything that is base, and urged the men to follow the good. At the end of his speech he gave the order to embark.

The whole fleet moved out and the barbarians immediately bore down on them. The Greeks backed away and came close to running up the beach, but then one Athenian ship surged forward and rammed a Persian. The two ships locked together and it was impossible for them to disengage, so the other Greeks came to the rescue of the Athenian ship and the battle began. According to the Athenians, this was how the battle began; the Aeginetans say that they struck the first blow. According to another story, the ghostly figure of a woman appeared; she called out orders in a voice loud enough for the whole fleet to hear and rebuked the Greeks in these words: 'Fools! How much further will you fall back?'

The Phoenicians were positioned on the right-hand end of the line, the end nearest Eleusis, opposite the Athenians. The Ionians were at the left-hand end, nearest Piraeus, facing the Lacedaemonians. A few of the Ionians fought half-heartedly as Themistocles had urged them to, but most of them fought well. However, the Persian fleet was very badly mauled, with the Athenians and the Aeginetans doing most of the damage. This was bound to be the outcome since the Greeks fought with discipline and in good order while the barbarians' efforts were without direction or control. Even so the Persian fleet fought much better than it had off Euboea. Every man tried his best for fear that Xerxes had his eye on him alone.

I cannot say with any precision how most individuals fought in the battle on either side. However, Queen Artemisia made the King think even more highly of her in this way: the Persian fleet was in complete chaos and Artemisia was being pursued by an Athenian ship. Her escape was blocked as there were friendly ships in her way and she was closest to the enemy. Thinking quickly, she rammed a friendly ship. The Athenian captain, thinking either that her ship must be Greek or that it was a deserter from the barbarian fleet, broke off the chase and turned on other ships.

85

This dirty trick impressed Xerxes greatly. He saw the incident and his staff, knowing Artemisia's flag well, assured him that the ship was hers. It was assumed the ship Artemisia had sunk was an enemy one, and by great good luck, none of the crew survived to accuse her of her crime. Xerxes' reaction to this was to say, 'My men have turned into women and my women have turned into men.'

In the struggle one of Xerxes' brothers, a general, died. Many other leading Persians and Medes died with him. Some Greeks were killed too, but only a few; the Greeks know how to swim and those who survived the hand-to-hand fighting when their ships went down were able to get back to Salamis. Many barbarians were drowned, however. The Persians lost most ships when their first line was driven back. This was because the ships behind were pressing forward to do their bit to impress the King and ran into those that were retreating.

In this chaos some Phoenicians who had lost their ships came before the King and blamed the Ionians for it, accusing them of treason. While they were speaking a Samothracian ship rammed an Athenian ship. While the Athenian ship was sinking, an Aeginetan ship rammed the Samothracian ship and sank it. But the Samothracians are javelin-fighters and they swept the deck of the ship that had sunk them with their javelins, boarded it and captured it. The Samothracians were originally from Ionia, so this saved the Ionians from punishment for treason, as Xerxes then turned on the Phoenicians and gave orders for them to be beheaded; he was full of bitterness and blaming everyone, and he certainly did not want cowards accusing better men of treason. Indeed, whenever Xerxes saw any of his ships achieve anything noteworthy as he watched the battle from his position on the hillside facing Salamis, he asked what ship it was. Then his scribes would write down the name of the ship's captain, the city he was from and who his father was.

So the rout of the Persians began. The Aeginetans were waiting for the barbarians as they tried to break out down the channel and back to Phaleron, and they did very well there. Meanwhile the Athenians battered away at the ships that still resisted or were trying to get away and the Aeginetans dealt with any that escaped the Athenians. The barbarian ships that survived the battle escaped to Phaleron and the protection of the army.

At this stage Themistocles' ship was pursuing one of the enemy and came alongside an Aeginetan ship. (This had just rammed a Sidonian ship, the one that sank the Aeginetan scout ship off Sciathos and took Pytheas prisoner. Pytheas, who had fought so heroically at Artemisium, was on board and this is how he got home to Aegina.) The Aeginetan captain recognised Themistocles' ship by the general's flag it flew and shouted out some rude remarks about the Athenians' accusations that Aegina was a friend of Persia.

The Athenians tell a story about Adimantus, the Corinthian general. At the beginning of the battle, they say, just as the two fleets were coming together, he was so terrified that he hoisted his sails and turned and ran. The rest of the Corinthians followed their general's example. But when they reached the top end of Salamis a boat met them; it was there by some divine providence because no mortal seems to have sent it. At this point the Corinthians did not know what was happening to the rest of the fleet, and this is why they talk of divine intervention. Anyway, as the boat and the ships drew near to each other, whoever was on the boat shouted, 'Adimantus, by turning your ships away in flight you are betraying the Greeks. But even now they are winning the victory they prayed for.' Adimantus did not believe this and then the people on the boat offered themselves as hostages, ready to die if the Greeks did not prove to be the victors. So Adimantus and the rest turned back and rejoined the fleet when the fighting was all over. That is the Athenians' story; the Corinthians say it is not true and claim that they played a leading part in the battle, and the rest of the Greeks support them in this.

Aristides, the Athenian, whose excellence I spoke of earlier, also played his part in the struggle. He led the force of Athenian hoplites that landed on the island of Psyttalea and killed all the Persians who were there.

When the battle was over the Greeks towed all the hulks that were still afloat to Salamis. They were ready to fight again, expecting the King to use the ships he had left. But Xerxes was afraid that the Greeks would sail to the Hellespont and break his bridges, cutting him off in Europe and putting him in danger of his life. So he planned to retreat.

The battle had begun with the Persians moving up the straits beyond the island of Psyttalea. They were probably in a column, several triremes abreast, and keeping to the Attic shore. The plan was to turn and form a line, either when the

Greeks moved out or when the column was opposite the Greek anchorages and beaches. The Phoenicians led the column and were on the right of the line when the turn was made; this was the place traditionally taken by the best troops in land-battles, and at sea. The Athenians were on the left and northern end of the Greek line. Their fleet was the largest and best but the position on the right was taken by the Spartans since they headed the Greek alliance.

The Greeks were ready for the Persians, united and determined. Themistocles had made sure of this. The more enemy ships they could draw into the straits the better. Herodotus mentions two tactics which may have been devised with this in mind. The first involved backing away from the advancing line after initially moving out to meet it. The second was the apparent flight of the Corinthian fleet. The sight of forty triremes under sail would have been evidence to the Persians that the allied fleet was breaking up and on the run. The suggestion that the Corinthians were actually trying to escape has a lot to do with the fact that Athens and Corinth were bitter enemies at the time Herodotus was doing his researches.

The Greek attack on the Persian line would have been a co-ordinated movement. Some ships would have rammed ahead of the rest and there must have been a number of claims to have been the ship that struck the first blow. The arguments were never settled because the Athenians and the Aeginetans, for example, could have been as much as two thousand yards (2 km) apart. (Each trireme in a line took up at least fifty feet (15 m) of water, allowing for its own width, including oars, and the need for clear water between itself and its neighbours.) Themistocles' plan had worked out perfectly, if Herodotus is correct in saying that the Persians suffered their greatest losses when their first line was driven back and became entangled with the second. This was the most important phase of the battle.

In the final phase the Greeks harried the Persians as they did their best to escape from the trap which the straits of Salamis had become. The Persians would never have sailed into the straits if they had expected such a reception. Herodotus is able to describe a few individual incidents in this final phase. He would have heard the stories about Artemisia, queen of his native city, at an early age and it is not surprising that she gets rather more attention than Halicarnassus' contribution to the war really merits.

It is important in any assessment of the Persians' losses,

which must have been considerable, to remember that the Greeks were probably satisfied with clearing the straits and did not pursue the Persians far beyond Psyttalea. Moreover, they expected to have to fight again on the following day. The Persians could have reinforced the ships that survived Salamis with those that had been positioned around the southern and western coast of the island and may still have had a larger number of battle-worthy ships than the Greeks. But they could not risk further losses on the scale of those they had just sustained. Perhaps they reckoned that the cost had already been too great. Greece could still be won, but next year and by the army. The Persian navy had failed.

AFTER THE BATTLE

Xerxes sent word of the defeat to Persia immediately. Nothing on earth travels faster than these Persian messengers. This is how it is done: there is a horse and rider stationed along the route for each day the journey will take, and neither snow, nor rain, nor heat, nor darkness prevents each rider covering his section with the greatest speed. The first one passes the despatch to the second, and the second to the third, and so on. It is just like the relay race the Greeks run with torches in honour of Hephaestus.

When Xerxes' first message, that he had taken Athens, reached Susa, over 2,000 miles (3,200 km) away, the Persians were so delighted that they scattered myrtle branches in the streets, burned incense, sacrificed, feasted and generally made merry. But the second message, coming hard on the heels of the first, put a stop to this. They all tore their clothes and shouted and wailed; they were inconsolable, and they all blamed Mardonius. The main cause of their grief was not so much the loss of the ships as fear for Xerxes. In fact, the Persians carried on in this way until the King was safely home.

Mardonius saw that Xerxes had taken the defeat very badly and guessed that he had decided to retreat. He also reckoned that he, Mardonius, would be punished for having persuaded the King to march against Greece. He therefore decided it was better to gamble on either conquering Greece himself or dying gloriously in a great adventure, though he thought the odds on the former were better. So he offered to stay behind with a picked force of 300,000 men from the so far undefeated army. Xerxes agreed to this and ordered Mardonius to choose the men he wanted, commanding him to match his words with deeds.

At nightfall, on the King's orders, the fleet sailed from Phaleron and headed for the Hellespont to guard the bridges for the King to cross. In the night the fleet passed close to some headlands on the west coast of Attica, mistook them for ships and scattered in all directions. It was some time before they discovered what they were running from, got back into formation and sailed on.

Next day the Greeks saw the Persian army was still in position and assumed that the fleet was still at Phaleron. They thought there was going to be another battle and prepared to defend themselves. But when they found out that the fleet had gone, they immediately decided to pursue it. They followed it as far as Andros without sighting it and then held a council. Themistocles proposed that they should continue their pursuit through the islands then make straight for the Hellespont and break the bridges. However, Eurybiades was against this; he said it was the worst possible thing to do as far as the safety of Greece was concerned. For, if the King were forced to stay in Europe, he would not sit around doing nothing. If he did nothing, he would achieve nothing, and he would not be able to get home either. Moreover, his army would starve. But, if the King worked at it, the whole of Europe might come over to his side, city by city and people by people, each one either being conquered by him or coming to terms. Then his men would be fed by each year's harvest. It was Eurybiades' opinion that the King would not stay in Europe after being defeated at sea and that he should therefore be allowed to make his escape; when he had returned to his own country the war could be carried into Asia. The rest of the Peloponnesian generals agreed with this proposal.

When Themistocles realised that he could not persuade a majority of the generals to sail to the Hellespont, he took a different line. He spoke to the Athenians in these words (the Athenians were very angry that the Persians had got away and were eager to sail on to the Hellespont even without the rest of the Greeks, if they would not come): 'I myself have come across this phenomenon on many occasions and have heard of it happening even more often – when driven into a corner beaten men will fight back and even regain what they have previously lost. Let us not pursue these beaten men. We have had the good fortune to save ourselves and Greece by driving off this swarm of enemies – and we did not achieve this unaided. For gods and heroes were with us; they thought Asia and Europe too much of a prize for one godless, impious king, a man who treats the property of gods and men alike, a man who burns and smashes down the statues of our gods, and even whips and fetters the ocean! All is well with us, so let us stay in Greece for now and care for ourselves and our families. Let us rebuild our houses and sow our fields. Our barbarian enemy is routed. Next spring we can sail for the Hellespont and Ionia.' Themistocles said all this to put the King in his debt so that he would have someone to turn to if he got into trouble with the Athenians (which, of course, did happen). The Athenians took his words at their face value and were persuaded. Themistocles already had a reputation for cleverness and now the Athenians thought he was both clever and wise, so they were ready to go along with whatever he said.

Themistocles immediately sent Sicinnus to Xerxes a second time. His message was this: 'Themistocles, the Athenian general, the best in all the Greek alliance, has sent me to tell you what he has done to help you – he has restrained the Greeks from pursuing you and from breaking your bridges across the Hellespont. Lead your army home, he says, no-one will hinder you.'

Having taken this decision not to pursue the Persian fleet or break the bridges, the Greeks besieged Andros. This was the first island Themistocles had demanded money from and he was refused. There was no end to his greed. He used the messengers he had sent to Xerxes to carry demands for money to the other islands. He threatened to bring the Greek fleet and besiege them as well, and by this means he collected large sums of money from Carystus and Paros. Both these islands had heard that Andros was under siege for supporting Persia and knew of Themistocles' great reputation as a general, so they were afraid and sent the money. I do not know for sure if other islands gave money, but it is likely they did. And, using Andros as his base, Themistocles collected all this money without the other generals knowing anything about it.

There is no reason to doubt the main facts in Herodotus' description of what happened after the battle, though his sources may have invented or embroidered the parts played by individuals. Some sort of message may have been sent to Xerxes, but it would certainly not have been taken by Sicinnus. There would have been a lot of discussion amongst the Greek generals about how far to pursue the Persian fleet but an expedition as far as the Hellespont would have been ruled out by the lateness of the season, if it was even considered. In fact Xerxes himself did not need his bridges to escape from Europe. For the Greeks, a brief cruise nearer home bases to raise some money and punish collaborators was the best use of time and resources before the autumn weather closed in. It is unlikely that Themistocles would have been able to use the money raised to line his own pockets secretly, so this anecdote is probably another example of prejudice against the man.

AESCHYLUS' 'THE PERSIANS'

The tragedian Aeschylus almost certainly watched the battle of Salamis and probably fought in it. *The Persians* was performed in Athens in 472, eight years after the battle, and includes a vivid description of the fighting.

A tragedy was an act of religion and poetry; it was not concerned with specific historical facts but with universal truths and problems – the will of the gods, man's relationship with the gods and with other men, human law against divine law, fate and free will. Most tragedies, therefore, took their themes from the legendary past or myths. But the conflict between the Greeks and the Persians was large enough and important enough to provide tragic themes, although it was so recent and close to home. It is the only surviving tragedy of this kind but the names of others are known and Herodotus mentions one of them – *The Destruction of Miletus* by Phrynichus.

Herodotus treats Xerxes as a tragic character, a great king whose actions, nobility and power offends the gods. Aeschylus' theme is the same but his tragedy also glorifies Athens. Religious convention did not allow him to name individual Athenians but no-one in the audience could fail to be reminded of Themistocles' part in the victory. The stirring battle-cry that Aeschylus' messenger reports may even be the final words of Themistocles' speech ('the best of all the speeches') before the Greeks embarked. But by 472 the Athenians had had enough of Themistocles. *The Persians* may have been part of the efforts of Themistocles and his supporters to strengthen his weakening political position. If it was, it did not work. Later in 472 Themistocles was ostracised. He spent the rest of his life serving Athens, first by doing what he could to check the growing power of Sparta, then in various dealings with Persia. He also looked after his own interests with characteristic shrewdness and efficiency!

The *Persians* is set in the Persian royal palace at Susa, and its main action is the arrival of the news of the defeat at Salamis and its impact on Xerxes' queen and council. The Chorus of Persian councillors opens the play, anxiously speculating about the fate of Xerxes' expedition. Queen Atossa then enters and tells them about the ominous dreams she has had.

Atossa	These dreams filled me with dread,
	And, speaking of them, I have made you tremble.
	For, know this well, if my son succeeds,
	He will be the wonder of the world.
	But if he fails –
	Well, then, he will be answerable to no city state.
	If he lives, he will still be King.
	But why does my son so long to win this prize?
Chorus	Because, if he wins Athens, he will win all Greece.
Atossa	And is Athens strong, well armed with fighting men?
Chorus	Strong indeed. Already she has done much harm to Persia.
Atossa	How else is Athens strong? Is the city rich?
Chorus	A rich spring, a stream of silver, flows from her soil.
Atossa	Are the Athenians masters of the bow?
Chorus	No, not at all; they fight with heavy spears and shields.
Atossa	And who shepherds them, who commands their host?
Chorus	Athenians are subject to no man; they are no master's slaves.
Atossa	How, then, can they resist invading enemies?
Chorus	Just as they beat back Darius' mighty army.
Atossa	These are your opinions and they will alarm
	The parents of the sons who went to fight.
Chorus	You will soon know if there is truth in them, I think.

A Messenger arrives

Messenger	Cities of Asia, land of Persia, haven of wealth!
	At one stroke your happiness is shattered.
	The flower of your manhood is fallen.
	Your fleet and army are destroyed.
	Persians, I can tell you this at first hand –

	I was there. I saw it all.
	The shores of Salamis are littered with dead.
	The headlands are draped with butchered corpses.
Chorus	Our friends and loved ones are sea-sodden,
	Wave-tossed corpses, washed to and fro by the waves!
Messenger	Our bows were useless. The whole fleet was destroyed,
	Crushed, ploughed under by the smashing rams.
	What name more vile to our ears than Salamis!
	Athens, the very word makes me weep!

[Having learned that Xerxes is safe but how many others have died, Atossa continues:]

Atossa	Your message means utter woe for Persia,
	Shame and bitter lamentations!
	But now go back over your tale:
	Tell how many Hellene ships there were,
	Daring to face the Persian fleet in battle,
	Ship to ship and ram to ram.
Messenger	The Persian fleet was stronger, I assure you,
	In numbers. The Greek fleet was three hundred strong
	Setting aside a special detachment of ten ships.
	Xerxes, I know, had a thousand warships under his command
	And two hundred and seven lighter vessels.
	Did we go into battle too weak in numbers?
	We did not – whatever god destroyed our fleet
	Tilted the balance with false weights.
	Gods watch over the city of the goddess Pallas.
Atossa	Then is Athens safe? Is the city not destroyed?
Messenger	As long as there are men to fight, a city's safe.
Atossa	How did the battle begin, then? Tell me.
	Who struck first? Was it the Greeks
	Or my son, rejoicing in the might of his fleet?
Messenger	It was some avenging power or evil spirit
	That swept us to disaster.
	A Greek came from the Athenian fleet
	To see your son and told him this:
	When night's dark mantle fell

94

The Greeks would wait no longer
But jump to their rowing benches and save them-
selves,
Secretly escaping, each to his own city.
This was a trick. The King did not see it.
He gave no thought to the envy of the gods
But sent this order to his captains:
When the sun's last rays had left the earth
They were to sail in three divisions
And blockade the straits and open sea.
Some were to draw a noose around the island
And, if any Greeks escaped their fated doom,
Death was to be the penalty.
This was your son's confident decree.
He knew not what the gods had planned.
Eager for battle, but without loss of discipline,
Our men ate their supper. Then each oarsman
Bound his oar to the well-worn pin.
The sun's light faded, down came the night,
And each man, master of his oar or weapons,
Went on board. Ship cheered ship.
Each moved to its position as commanded
And spent the night at sea, following the captains'
orders.
The night went by. The Greek fleet made no move.
Then dawn came on its white-maned steed
Lighting the earth with beauty
And a great cry lifted from the Hellene ranks,
A triumph song, echoing from the island rocks.
Fear chilled Persian hearts, fear and shattered
expectations.
The Greeks who sang this paean were not defeated
But thrusting into battle with spirits high.
Trumpets blazed along their line
And all in time their oar-blades beat the waves.
Suddenly we could see the whole fleet,
The right wing leading in perfect order, then the
rest.
A great shout went up, dinning on our ears.
'Sons of Hellas, forward to freedom!
Freedom for the country of your birth.
Freedom for your children and your wives!

Freedom for the shrines of your ancestral gods!
Freedom for the tombs of your fathers!
Fight! Now all is at stake!'
From our side a hubbub of Persian voices sounded
back.
There was no delaying now.
Ship struck ship with brazen prow.
The first into action was Greek,
Shattering a Phoenician's stern, but the rest soon
followed.
At first sheer weight held the Persian line together,
But we were no help to each other,
Packed as we were in a narrow space.
Ship smashed ship with clashing bronze,
And oars and timber splintered.
With skilful steering the Greeks closed the trap.
Ships rolled over. Soon the sea was hidden;
Corpses and wreckage clogged the swell
And dead festooned the rocks and beaches.
Then our whole fleet broke and ran.
The Greeks hacked and stabbed at any survivors
With broken spars, like fishermen with a great catch
of tunny.
Shrieks and wails rang out across the water
Until night and darkness brought an end.
Such horror! If I spoke for ten full days
I could not fully describe it.
But of this you can be certain – in one day
Never have so many died.

The messenger's speech can be treated as an eye-witness
account of the battle which must have agreed with the
Athenian audience's memories and beliefs about Salamis. But
it was written for dramatic impact, not as a historical
reconstruction, and it was also written from the Persian point
of view. The messenger who brought the first news of the
defeat to Susa would not have taken part in the battle or seen
it. The Persians could not have heard any words the Greeks
might have chanted or shouted before the two fleets closed
together. The numbers for the Greek fleet may be accurate, if
reduced a little for effect; the Persian numbers are certainly
greatly inflated. But the impression of the battle is very
convincing. First there is the shock and disappointment of the

Persians' realisation that they faced solid and determined resistance. If each fleet was drawn up with a friendly shore behind it (a good argument for the interpretation of the opening phase of the battle adopted here), the Greek right flank would have advanced ahead of the rest in order to close Themistocles' trap by putting pressure on the Persians left and southernmost flank. If this is what happened the first blow is likely to have been struck at that end of the line, but remember, Aeschylus was writing for an Athenian audience. The main phase of the battle in which the Greeks effectively strangled the Persian fleet is graphically described and the extract ends with the butchery that followed.

The messenger then has a few lines on Aristides' successful action on the island of Psyttalea and goes on to describe the horrors of Xerxes' retreat. Atossa and the Chorus lament all this suffering and call up the ghost of Darius from his tomb. Darius grieves over his son's folly in challenging the gods and prophesies the disaster to come at the battle of Plataea. The tragedy ends with the return of Xerxes, miserable and bedraggled.

9   Autumn 480 to Spring 479

AUTUMN 480

> Xerxes went home. Some of the men with him, especially any
> stragglers, would have suffered on the forced march. But
> isolated incidents, reported from different points along the
> route, were built up into a tale of general disaster. However,
> the Persians still controlled most of the land they passed
> through and the force that escorted Xerxes to the Hellespont
> was strong enough to besiege two powerful cities once the
> King was safely out of Europe. Meanwhile, the Greeks shared
> out the spoils of victory but were unable to agree on the
> honours due to their leaders. However, the Spartans were
> more generous and in Sparta Themistocles received the
> honours he deserved.

A few days after the battle of Salamis, Xerxes' army began its
retreat. Mardonius decided to escort the King. The campaigning season was over and he thought it best to spend the
winter in Thessaly and make his attack on the Peloponnese
the following Spring. In Thessaly Mardonius picked out the
men he wanted. He began with the Immortals (except for
Hydarnes, their commander, who would not leave the King).
To them he added the most heavily armed of the rest of the
Persians and the best of their cavalry, a thousand strong. He
chose all the Medes, Sacae, Bactrians and Indians in the
army, both foot soldiers and cavalry. Finally he picked out a
few men from each of the other national contingents, either
for their looks or because of the good service he knew they
had already given. The Persians in their necklaces and bracelets made up the largest part of the force, though the Medes
were almost equal to them in number but less than their

98

equals as fighters. In all Mardonius had a force of 300,000 men.

At about this time the Delphic oracle instructed the Lacedaemonians to demand compensation from Xerxes for Leonidas' death and see what answer he gave. The Spartans sent a herald immediately and he arrived in Thessaly before the Persian army divided. He was taken into the King's presence and said, 'King of the Persians, the Lacedaemonians and the Spartan sons of Heracles demand reparations for their dead King, slain by you while he defended Greece.'

The King laughed long and hard, then he pointed to Mardonius who happened to be standing near him and said, 'This is Mardonius. He will pay the reparations due to them.' The herald had his answer and left.

The Greeks, meanwhile, moved on to Carystus, devastated it and then returned to Salamis. There they set aside the 'first fruits' of the spoils of battle for the gods and divided the rest amongst themselves. After this they sailed to the Isthmus to vote who was to receive the hero's prize for his part in the fighting. When the time came to vote, each general went up to the altar of Poseidon and voted for himself, but most of them cast their second vote for Themistocles. So nobody received more than one vote for the first prize but Themistocles got far more votes than anyone else for the second prize. Jealousy prevented the Greeks reaching any decision about the award and they all sailed home leaving the issue unsettled. But Themistocles' name was on everybody's lips and all Greece thought him much the best of the generals.

Themistocles went off to Sparta in search of the honour that was his due, but had been denied him by the Greeks who had fought at Salamis. He was made very welcome and received many honours. Eurybiades was crowned with an olive wreath for his heroism, but Themistocles was awarded a crown for his wisdom and his skilful generalship and given the finest chariot in Sparta as a gift. Then he was sent on his way with many speeches and escorted as far as the Tegean border by the special detachment of three hundred Spartans known as the Knights. No-one else I know of has ever been honoured in this way by the Spartans.

There was a man at Athens called Timodemus whose only claim to fame was his hatred of Themistocles. Bitter with envy, he made a violent speech attacking Themistocles and his visit to Sparta, arguing that the honours he had received were not intended for him personally but for Athens. He went on in this vein for some time until Themistocles said, 'I agree with you – if I came from the farthest corner of Attica, I would not have been honoured by the Spartans. But you, sir, are from Athens and the Spartans would never honour you!' That was the end of that argument.

WINTER

Early in 479 Mardonius tried to tempt the Athenians out of the Greek alliance using Alexander, King of Macedon and an ancestor of Alexander the Great, as his ambassador. With the Athenians on their side or neutral, the Persians would control the sea and win the war. In this episode Herodotus depicts the Athenians appealing to the ideals of Greece and their Peloponnesian allies' better instincts.

During the winter Mardonius sent a man round Greece to consult all the oracles on his behalf. Perhaps he was advised by them to try and make an alliance with Athens. Anyway, he sent Alexander, King of Macedon, to Athens. He chose him to be his messenger because his sister was married to a Persian and because of his well-established diplomatic ties with Athens and the good services he had done the city; Mardonius thought he could achieve an alliance with the Athenians through Alexander. He wanted this because he knew they were a brave and powerful race and had been chiefly responsible for the disaster which had overtaken the Persians at Salamis. He hoped friendship with Athens would give him mastery of the sea, and it certainly would have done that; on land he thought his strength was far superior anyway. So this was how he reckoned he could make sure of victory in Greece.

Alexander came to Athens and made this speech: 'Athenians, these are the words of Mardonius: "I have had a message from the King which runs – I forgive the Athenians all the wrong they have done me. Mardonius, you are to do the following: give back to the Athenians their land and let them choose more for themselves, wherever they want it; rebuild for them the temples I burned down. Do these things on condition that the Athenians make terms with me – I, Mardonius, must carry out the King's command; if I do not it will be you Athenians who prevented me."

'Speaking for myself, I, Alexander, beg you to accept these

terms. It is clear to me that you can't keep up a war against Xerxes indefinitely. If you had seemed capable of it, I would never have come to you with such a proposal. But the King's power is super-human and his arm is very long. I fear for you if you do not accept these favourable terms now, while they are available to you. For in all the Greek alliance no-one is more directly in the path of the war or more certain of destruction – the battleground is already marked out in your country.

'Accept the terms; it is an immense honour that the Great King does you, to choose to forgive you alone of all the Greeks and make you his friends.'

The Spartans knew about Alexander's mission. They were very much afraid that the Athenians would agree to the Persians' terms and therefore decided to send ambassadors of their own. They were called before the same assembly as Alexander. The Athenians delayed things to bring this about because they wanted to make their feelings quite clear to the Lacedaemonians.

When Alexander had finished it was the Spartans' turn to speak. They said, 'We have been sent to beg you not to harm Greece or listen to any offers from the barbarians. For any Greek to do this would be a crime. But for you it would be worst of all. There are many reasons. You stirred up this war which we did not want. Only your land was at stake at first, but now all Greece is involved. Apart from that, it is an intolerable thought that you Athenians, who have given freedom to so many, should be responsible for the enslavement of Greeks.

'Even so, we sympathise with you. You have lost one harvest and will lose another and your homes and property are in ruins. To compensate you we bring you an offer from the Lacedaemonians and their allies – we will take care of your women and all other non-combatants for as long as the war lasts.

'Do not let Alexander persuade you with his polished delivery of Mardonius' message. What else would he say? He is a tyrant collaborating with a tyrant! Do not let him persuade you if you are in your right minds; you know you cannot trust barbarians, or believe what they say.'

The Athenians gave Alexander his answer first. 'We know that the King's power is many times greater than ours – you don't need to tell us that! But we love freedom and we will defend ourselves to the limits of our ability. Don't you try to persuade us to agree terms with the Persians – we never will. Tell Mardonius that the Athenians say this: as long as the sun keeps its course in the sky we will never agree terms with Xerxes. We will come out and fight him, trusting in our allies, the gods and heroes whom he scorns, whose shrines and effigies he burned.

'To you, Alexander, we have this to say: never again appear before us with such a message. Never again try to advise us to act against what is right and think you are doing us a service. We like you and you have been a good friend to this city; we do not want you to suffer anything unpleasant at Athenian hands.'

Then the Athenians gave the Spartan ambassadors their answer. 'Human nature makes the Lacedaemonians fear that we will agree terms with the Persians. But your fear does the Athenians a grave injustice. Not all the gold on earth, no gift of land, however beautiful or rich, could persuade us to join with Persia and enslave Greece. Many powerful reasons prevent us doing this, even if it was what we wanted to do. Most important, we must avenge the destruction of the images of our gods and their temples. We cannot make a treaty with the man who committed these crimes! And then, we Athenians cannot betray the Greek blood, the language, the religion we share, the Greek way of life which binds us all together. We tell you, if you do not know it already, there will be no treaty with Xerxes as long as there is a single Athenian living.

'We sincerely thank you for the consideration you show in offering to look after our families and households for as long as our homes are in ruins. This is great generosity. However, we will look after ourselves as best we can and not be a burden to you.

'All that is settled. Now send your army as quickly as you can. We reckon the Persians will soon be attacking us, as soon as they hear that we will not do what they want. We should immediately march to meet them in Boeotia, before they arrive in Attica.' This was the message the ambassadors took back to Sparta.

SPRING 479

When Alexander returned with the Athenians' answer, Mardonius immediately began the march from Thessaly to Athens. He raised troops in all the countries he passed through and the ruling families of Thessaly gave him their support. When he reached Boeotia the Thebans tried to persuade him to halt, arguing that there was no better place for his army to stay and that he could win Greece from there without advancing any further or striking a blow. In their view it would be difficult for even the whole of the rest of the world to overcome Greece by force, as long as the Greek alliance held together. They advised him to send bribes to the men in positions of power in each city and to destroy the alliance in that way.

Mardonius did not follow the Thebans' advice. His greatest wish was to take Athens a second time. Partly it was a matter of pride; partly it was because he planned to inform the King in Sardis that Athens was in his hands by means of a chain of beacons across the islands of the Aegean. When he arrived in Attica he discovered that the Athenians had gone and that most of them were with the fleet on Salamis. So the city was deserted when he took it. Ten months had passed since Athens was taken the first time by the King.

The Athenians had stayed on the mainland for as long as they could, waiting for an army to come from the Peloponnese to support them. But when the Peloponnesians kept on delaying sending help and news came that the Persians had entered Boeotia, the Athenians crossed to Salamis with everything they could carry. They sent messages to Sparta rebuking the Peloponnesians for standing by and letting the Persians invade Attica instead of coming out to meet them in Boeotia. They also reminded them of the rewards they had been promised by the Persians if they changed sides and made it clear that they would think of some way of looking after their own interests if they had no help from the Peloponnesians.

As it happened, the Lacedaemonians were celebrating the festival of Hyacinthus at this time, and paying due respect to the god came first as far as they were concerned. Also they had not quite completed the wall they were building across the Isthmus.

On reaching Athens Mardonius sent an ambassador across to Salamis repeating the offer that he had made to the Athenians through Alexander. He was well aware that the Athenians were no more inclined to be friendly than before. But he made this second attempt in the hope that their stubborn resolution would be weakened now that Attica lay under the shadow of his spear.

Mardonius' ambassador came before the council and delivered his message. One councillor, Lycidas, favoured accepting Mardonius' offer and putting it to the vote in the assembly. (This man was either bribed or really liked the idea!) But the other councillors were very angry at this suggestion and so were the rest of the Athenians when they heard about it. In fact they stoned Lycidas to death, though they let Mardonius' ambassador return unharmed. The island was in uproar. When the Athenian women heard what had happened they gathered together, each passing the word on to her neighbour, and made their way to Lycidas' house and stoned his wife and children to death. This was a completely spontaneous act.

When the Ephors, the chief Spartan ministers, received the Athenians' message they put off answering for a day, then for another day and delayed answering for ten days in all. Meanwhile the Peloponnesian allies were working flat out on the wall across the Isthmus and it was nearly finished. I do not know why the Spartans were so worried that the Athenians would go over to the Persians when Alexander visited them, if they were so unconcerned now. Perhaps they thought they no longer needed the Athenians on their side once they had fortified the Isthmus.

Anyway, in the end the Spartans gave their answer and finally took the field. A man from Tegea, one of Lacedaemonia's most influential foreign residents, found out from the Ephors what the Athenians' message was and the story is that he persuaded them to do what the Athenians asked them to do just before they were to give the ambassadors their final audience. 'If the Athenians become our enemies and allies of the Persians, the Peloponnese will be laid wide open however strongly you fortify the Isthmus,' he argued. 'You must listen to the Athenians or they may change their minds and do great harm to Greece.'

This advice was taken to heart. The Ephors said nothing to the Athenian ambassadors, but gave order that 5,000 Spartans, each with seven helots (peasant slaves) in attendance, should set out before dawn the next day. Pausanias, son of Cleombrotus, was in command of them.

Next day the Athenians came for their audience, fully intending to abandon their mission and go home. In their parting speech they threatened to make an alliance with Xerxes. Then the Spartans told them that an army was already on the way. The Athenians were amazed and started their journey home immediately. Another 5,000 hoplites from the country districts of Lacedaemonia set off at about the same time.

The Argives had promised Mardonius that they would prevent the Spartans leaving Lacedaemonia. But when they heard that Pausanias was on the march they sent their best long-distance runner to Attica with a message for Mardonius. This was to inform him that the Lacedaemonian army was on the move and that they, the Argives, could not do anything to stop it.

Mardonius marched into Attica and occupied Athens again to put more pressure on the Athenians. The Peloponnesians were clearly reluctant to advance beyond the Isthmus, as usual, and Herodotus may have allowed a note of scorn to creep in here. Evacuated to Salamis once again and temporarily isolated, the Athenians might, Mardonius hoped, be more easily persuaded this time. Possibly the violent and 'spontaneous' reaction which Herodotus describes was intended to discourage a small but dangerous minority; Lycidas was unlikely to have been the only Athenian who felt the Persian offer was worth considering.

Finally the Spartans decided to move. Their festival was over, the wall across the Isthmus was complete and the Athenians, they knew, were about to make public use of their ultimate bargaining point – the threat of withdrawal with their fleet from the Greek alliance. The Spartans probably had no intention of deserting the Athenians but simply wanted to act in their own time. They might even have got some dry amusement out of the Athenians' increasingly desperate pleading! The wall at the Isthmus was important because it was to be the next line of defence. If it was going to be needed, Athens would by then be out of the war, and the Peloponnesians who had not joined the alliance might well have become their enemies. But the Spartans, at least, would have resisted to the inevitable end. In any case when they acted, the Spartans acted decisively and the final victory depended on them.

Mardonius decided not to stay in Attica any longer. Up till now he had taken no action because he wanted to know what the Athenians were going to do. He had not harmed the land of Attica in any way in the hope that they would, at last, agree terms. But when persuasion had failed and he had discovered what the true situation was, he set fire to Athens and flattened anything that was still standing – fortifications, private houses and temples. Then he retreated, leaving Attica before Pausanias' army reached the Isthmus. He made this move because Attica is the wrong sort of country for cavalry operations and because if he had wanted to retreat after being defeated in battle, the only escape route would have been a narrow pass which could be closed by a small force. His plan was to fall back on Thebes and fight there in good cavalry country with a friendly city behind him.

Although the Thebans were on his side, Mardonius had all their trees cut down when he reached their territory. This was not an act of hostility; he needed to build a fortified camp to protect his army in case things did not turn out as he intended. The Persian front line stretched along the north bank of the river Asopus from a point opposite Erythrae westwards as far as the northern edge of the Plataean plain. The stockade was not as long as this; each of its sides measured about a mile and a quarter (2 km). Mardonius had contingents with him from all the surrounding Greek cities that had sided with Persia and they had all joined him in his march on Athens, except for the Phocians who were there because they had been forced to come.

Meanwhile, the Lacedaemonians had set up camp at the Isthmus. The rest of the Peloponnesians (those who chose the better course of action) joined them there when they saw that the Spartans had gone to war; they felt it would not be right to stay behind. The omens were good and the entire force marched to Eleusis. The Athenians crossed over from Salamis and joined the Greek army there. They sacrificed again and once more the omens were favourable, so they marched on to Erythrae in Boeotia. There they found the enemy in position along the Asopus and took up positions facing them along the foothills of Mount Cithaeron.

As for the Persian fleet, it had spent the winter at Cyme after ferrying the King and the men with him across the Hellespont. At the first breath of spring it assembled at Samos. Because of the damage suffered at Salamis, the fleet sailed no further west than Samos. It remained there, three hundred ships in all, guarding against a second rebellion in Ionia. The Persians reckoned the Greeks would not sail as far as Ionia but would be content to defend their own territory. They based this assessment on the fact that the Greeks had not pursued them after Salamis but had been glad to be rid of them. The Persian navy was, in fact, completely demoralised, but the Persians thought Mardonius would win an easy victory with the army. So the fleet stayed at Samos and the generals planned what they could do to harass the enemy from there while they waited for news from Mardonius.

The coming of spring and Mardonius' presence in Thessaly had roused the Greeks to action on the sea and a fleet of about 110 ships had assembled at Aegina. Leutychides, a Spartan of royal blood, was in command. Messengers arrived from Ionia, begging the Greeks to sail there, but they would only go as far as Delos, and they were reluctant even to do that. They were afraid of what lay beyond since they had no idea what might be there. They thought the whole area was occupied by the Persians; Samos seemed as remote as the Pillars of Heracles. As it happened, the Persians were too demoralised to dare sail further west than Samos, while the Greeks dared not do what the Ionians requested and sail further east than Delos. Fear patrolled the sea between them!

Mardonius moved back to Thebes into Boeotia for good tactical reasons. At this time, according to Herodotus, Persian forces reached as far west as they were ever to go into Europe; Herodotus either forgot the story about the force that went to Delphi, or did not believe it! Up till now the Greek and Persian fleets had kept their distance. The Greek fleet was not much more than a quarter of the size of the one that had fought at Salamis because the manpower was needed to face the Persians on land. But when the right moment came it sailed east. The larger Persian fleet could not sail west because the Ionians were becoming restless again. Herodotus' interpretation of the situation at sea is perhaps over-dramatic, but the scene is set on the Greek mainland and in the Aegean for the two battles that decided the war.

10 The battle of Plataea

The Greeks and the Persians were facing each other across the river Asopus. The Persians were spread out along the north bank with their large fortified camp positioned to command the main roads running to Thebes. The Greek line was probably close to the rocky base of Mount Cithaeron, along the road that ran parallel to it linking the villages of Erythrae and Hysiae with the town of Plataea; Plataea had been destroyed by the Persians the year before.

The fighting at Plataea was spread out over several days. The Greek army totalled almost 40,000 hoplites with thousands of light-armed soldiers in support. The Persian army may have been somewhat larger but could not have been anywhere near the strength Herodotus claims for it. If it had been 350,000 strong the Greeks would have been swamped, especially in the middle stage of the battle, and would probably not have advanced to meet it at all. The fighting had three distinct phases and involved large-scale manoeuvres over a rectangle of land approximately eight miles (12 km) wide by four miles (6 km) deep.

The difficulties Herodotus would have faced in his attempt to record this battle were even greater than the problems presented by the battle of Salamis. The shape of the battle seems clear enough in outline but there are many important questions about it which can never be decisively answered. Details which would have been useful to the contemporary reader, like place-names or features of the landscape, are not so helpful today because several of them cannot now be identified with certainty. Physical features like gullies, banks, clumps of trees, hedges and riverbeds, which may have played an important part in the fighting, probably do not now exist so present-day maps or on-the-spot research cannot help much. Finally, Herodotus was able to take it for granted that his readers understood what battles were like and how they were fought in the fifth century. His readers were much better equipped than we are to relive this great victory through Herodotus' words, and Herodotus' main purpose was to enable them to do this. Their interests were different from the interests of historians today. Various stages in the battle can be identified in Herodotus' continuous narrative in this chapter.

Each stage of the battle is followed by an interpretation of what happened; other interpretations are possible!

THE BATTLEFIELD

From the Greek front line, close to the base of Mount Cithaeron, the ground fell away into the plain. The river and the Persians were about two miles (3–4 km) away. To the left of the Greek line, a low ridge, connecting a series of small hills, brought the higher ground closer to the river (the Greeks moved onto this ridge later in the battle). Normally hoplites were drawn up in eight rows so the Greek line would have been about three miles (4–5 km) in length. The formation probably was not a straight line but roughly followed the foothills. It may have been extended by screens of light-armed troops on each flank. The Persian line followed the river and was as long as or longer than the Greek line.

Mardonius had chosen the river plain as his battlefield. Attica was too hilly and enclosed for his purposes. The coastal plains behind Eleusis and Megara were spacious enough, but the narrow passes over Cithaeron could turn them into dangerous traps if he needed to retreat. An attack on the Isthmus wall was ruled out by the threat of an attack on his flank or rear launched by the Athenians from Salamis. The plains on either side of the Asopus gave Mardonius the ground and the space he needed for the fluid hit-and-run tactics to which his Asian forces and Greek cavalry were best suited. There were also good lines of retreat and a large friendly city, Thebes, behind him. Here the Persians were far enough south to draw the Peloponnesians out from behind their fortifications. The Peloponnesians recognised the need for a decisive battle as well as Mardonius did, and Mardonius' efforts to separate Athens from the Greek alliance would also have been an important factor.

Both sides had the same objective; to meet the enemy on as favourable terms as possible and win a decisive victory. For both sides supplies could be a problem and for both there was the fear of disunity and division in the ranks and the danger of potential enemies in the rear. Neither force could face the other indefinitely although stalemate was always a possibility. This was because the Greeks needed to maintain a solid line which

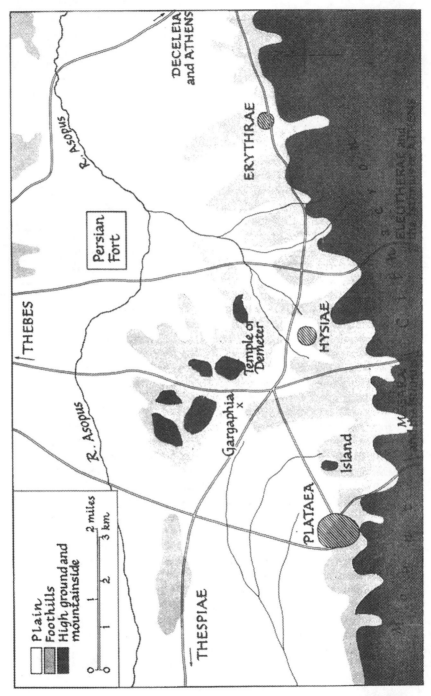

4 Plataea

could only be attacked from the front. The Persians on the other hand, knew that they had no chance of winning by frontal attacks; they needed to catch the Greeks moving, out in the open plain and preferably not in formation. Mardonius had a powerful force of Greek hoplites in his army, but obviously they were not enough to make a Greek-style battle feasible.

THE ARMIES

The Persian army was mostly armed and equipped as described by Herodotus on page 38. There were also Greeks in it. Some were hoplites and light-armed soldiers like the Greeks they faced, but there were also horsemen from Boeotia and northern Greece, who were more heavily armed than the Asian cavalry and who fought with lances as well as with javelins. The Asians, on the other hand, fought only with bows and javelins. For them a cavalry charge did not normally involve direct contact with the enemy.

Hoplite weapons and armour are described on page 21. Greek light-armed soldiers wore no armour. Javelins were their main weapon but they also carried swords and light shields. They were, for the most part, less well armed than the best Asian troops. But they could be used effectively in circumstances or on ground where the hoplite line's lack of mobility was a disadvantage. The light-armed soldiers who accompanied the Spartans were helots, peasant slaves. But in other Greek armies the light-armed troops were from the same poorer class of citizens that provided the navies with oarsmen.

FIRST PHASE

The Greeks made no move down onto the plain so Mardonius sent all his cavalry against them. Masistius, a famous cavalry commander, led them on a magnificent charger wth a golden bridle and beautiful trappings. The Persian cavalry attacked the Greeks squadron by squadron and did a lot of damage, and insulted them by calling them women.

The Megarians were unlucky enough to be in the most vulnerable position and were very hard pressed. They sent an urgent request to the Greek generals for help. Pausanias called for volunteers to replace the Megarians and only the Athenians were willing. They sent a picked force of three hundred hoplites and their archers. The position was out in front of the rest of the Greek army, and the engagement lasted a long time. The Persians continued to charge in squadrons and Masistius was always at their head. But then an arrow hit his horse in its side and it reared up in pain and threw him. The Athenians were onto him instantly. They caught his horse and Masistius died fighting. It proved very difficult to finish him off; under his purple tunic he wore golden scale-armour which resisted all blows until someone managed to spear him in the eye.

Masistius' men failed to see all this and they wheeled round and rode back, unaware that their commander had fallen. They only missed him when they regrouped for the next charge and found there was no one giving orders. Then they organised themselves and all charged together to win Masistius' body back.

Seeing the Persians attacking in full force instead of in squadrons, the Athenians called for help. Until the others arrived the fighting round the body was fierce. Without support the three hundred Athenians had a very hard time and came close to retreating. But when the rest of the Greeks came to their aid, the Persian cavalry had to give way and abandon Masistius, and many other horsemen fell around him. They retreated about a quarter of a mile (400 m) and discussed what they should do. As they now had no leader, they decided to ride back to Mardonius.

Mardonius and the rest of the army went into the deepest mourning for Masistius. They shaved their heads and even cut the manes off their horses and baggage animals, and lamented long and bitterly. The whole of Boeotia rang with lamentations for the death of a man more respected in Persia than anyone but Mardonius and the King.

While the Persians were honouring the dead Masistius in customary fashion, the Greeks were in good spirits because they had held and repulsed the Persian cavalry. They laid out Masistius' corpse on a wagon and paraded it along their line, and it was certainly worth looking at because he was a large and handsome man. All along the line the Greeks broke ranks to gaze at Masistius.

After this the Greeks decided to move downhill towards Plataea. The ground there was much better for an encampment than at Erythrae, and in particular was better supplied with water. So they made their way along the lower slopes of Mount Cithaeron past Hysiae and onto Plataean land. They took up new positions there on the level ground and low hills around the spring of Gargaphia.

When the order of battle was being worked out there was a violent argument between the Athenians and the Tegeans. Each claimed the position of honour on the flank not held by the Spartans, justifying their claim with references to their achievements, both in recent times and long ago. The argument was settled by a great shout from the whole army acclaiming the Athenians most worthy of the flank position.

It seems that the Persians did not oppose the Greeks as they came down from Mount Cithaeron and took up their positions. Perhaps Mardonius wanted to ensure the battle was decisive by taking on the entire Greek army. By the time the last men had come down onto the foothills, the first (the Spartans leading and on the right) would have been firmly into their defensive positions. Perhaps he was also hoping the Greeks would move further forward onto the plain.

Mardonius had made the first positive move when he saw that the Greeks were staying on the higher ground in front of Erythrae. He knew his cavalry would unsettle the Greeks and he may have hoped he could provoke them into a reaction that would give him the opportunity for a full-scale attack. The Megarians must have been out on a spur with gently sloping approaches to make their position so vulnerable. It suited the Athenians' pride to be remembered as volunteering to go to their aid. In fact they were positioned close to the Megarians in the order of battle and their company of archers, seemingly the only archers on the Greek side, made them the obvious choice. The archers were more important in this action than the 300 hoplites who escorted and screened them. However, the 3,000 Megarians would have welcomed both archers and hoplites as reinforcements.

Encouraged by their victory over the cavalry the Greeks decided to move forward and to the left along the ridge of foothills that separated Plataea and the plain in front of the town from the river. This is a difficult move to interpret. Good use of physical features and light-armed troops may have closed any gap between the Spartans on the right near the spring of Gargaphia and the base of the mountain, but the left flank appears to have been dangerously open. Perhaps Pausanias now wanted to provoke an attack. Certainly the Greeks made no attempt to cross the river but, according to Herodotus, Mardonius was not immediately provoked, either

113

by the movement, which must have taken some hours to complete, or by the apparent weakness of the new position.

ORDERS OF BATTLE

At this point Herodotus gives each side's order of battle. He describes in detail how Mardonius lined his forces up opposite the Greeks and implies that the two lines were equal in length. The number of Mardonius' Asian forces is a vague and highly unlikely total and, when giving his impossible figure of 50,000 for the Greeks in his army, Herodotus comments disarmingly 'that they were not counted'. Mardonius' tactics suggest that he had considerably fewer than 350,000 men under his command at Plataea. The numbers for the different contingents of hoplites in the Greek army, on the other hand, are likely to be reasonably accurate. Herodotus would have known how many hoplites each city represented at Plataea could muster in the middle of the fifth century. Numbers in 479 would not have been greatly different.

To the 38,700 hoplites in the Greek army Herodotus adds an enormous total of nearly 70,000 light-armed men. Almost half of them came with the 5,000 Spartans and, Herodotus points out, all 35,000 of these were equipped to fight. This suggests that not all the rest were armed. Some light-armed men may have played an important part in the actual fighting but Herodotus does not mention it. In any case a large proportion of them was probably used to escort and help carry the stream of supplies that had to be sent up from the Isthmus and, perhaps, also from Megara and Salamis.

SECOND PHASE

The next day, when they had made their dispositions, both sides offered sacrifices. The omens were good for the Greeks, providing they stayed on the defensive and did not make the first move by crossing the Asopus. And the omens were the same for Mardonius – unfavourable if he attacked, but good if he fought a defensive battle.

Eight days passed and all the time a steady stream of new arrivals was swelling the Greek ranks. Then one of the Thebans advised Mardonius that if he patrolled the trails leading down from Mount Cithaeron he would cut off many of the reinforce-

MARDONIUS' ARMY   THE GREEK ARMY

MARDONIUS' ARMY	THE GREEK ARMY
PERSIANS	11,500 consisting of 5,000 Spartans, 5,000 Lacedaemonians and 1,500 Tegeans
MEDES	8,900 including 5,000 Corinthians and 3,000 Sicyonians
BACTRIANS	3,400 including 1,000 each from Troezene and Phlius
INDIANS	1,300
SACAE	2,000
GREEKS consisting of hoplites from Boeotia, Locris, Malis, Phocis, Macedonia and Thessaly	11,600 consisting of 3,000 Megarians, 600 Plataeans and 8,000 Athenians

ments that were coming in daily. Mardonius thought this was good advice and sent off the cavalry. The operation was successful. They caught a convoy of 500 ox-carts carrying food to the army from the Peloponnese as it came out onto the plain. They slaughtered the beasts and their drivers indiscriminately until they had had enough of killing. Then they rounded up the remnants and drove them to Mardonius' camp.

For another two days both sides avoided battle. The Persians advanced as far as the river to see how the Greeks reacted but nobody crossed. However, Mardonius' cavalry continued to harass the Greeks and caused them great problems. The Thebans were giving the Persians whole-hearted support and repeatedly guided the horsemen into action, at which point the Persians and Medes would take over and demonstrate their fighting ability.

On the eleventh day, when there had been no new development except for a further increase in the Greeks' numbers, Mardonius began to worry about the delay. He discussed it with Artabazus, one of the few men whose advice Xerxes valued. Artabazus strongly recommended striking camp immediately and moving the whole army behind the walls of Thebes. There they had a large stockpile of provisions for the men and fodder for the animals, and large amounts of gold and silver in bullion, coins and plate. All they needed to do was sit quietly in Thebes and send generous gifts all over Greece, concentrating especially on the leading men in each city. The Greeks would soon sell their liberty without the Persians having to take any risks in battle. The Thebans agreed with this and thought Artabazus' prediction was accurate. Mardonius, however, took a more forceful but less sensible line; he completely disagreed. He thought the Persian army was much stronger than the Greek army. They should attack immediately and not stand by and watch the Greek army growing larger and larger. As for the sacrifices, they should ignore them and stop trying to force the right answer out of them. He wanted to get into battle in traditional Persian style.

Nobody spoke against Mardonius' proposal and his suggestion was adopted. After all, the King had put Mardonius, not Artabazus, in command of his army. So he gave orders for preparations to be made and for everything to be organised in readiness for the battle that the next day's dawn would bring.

In the middle of the night when all seemed quiet and both camps were deeply asleep Alexander, king of Macedon, rode up

116

to an Athenian outpost and asked to speak to their generals. He named them all but did not say who he was. The generals came out to meet him and this is what he said, 'Athenians, Mardonius and his army have failed to get favourable omens from their sacrifices. If they had succeeded, you would have been in battle days ago. But now Mardonius intends to ignore the omens and will attack at first light. I think he is worried that your numbers will increase even more, so be prepared. If Mardonius postpones his attack yet again, wait patiently; he only has enough supplies for a few days.

'If you are finally successful in this war, remember me and think what you can do to preserve my liberty. I am taking this great risk in revealing Mardonius' plans to you and saving you from an unexpected attack because I love Greece. I am Alexander, the Macedonian.' He then rode back to the Persian lines and returned to his position. The Athenian generals went over to the Spartan position on the right flank and told Pausanias what Alexander had told them.

Mardonius began the day by sending in his cavalry. They rode up to the Greek line and caused casualties all along it with their javelins and arrows, and, because they were mounted archers, the Greeks could not get to grips with them. They also fouled the stream from which the entire army got its water and choked it up. The Lacedaemonian contingent was the only one near the spring. All the rest were some distance from it but closer to the river Asopus. However, they had to take their water from the spring because the Persian cavalry's arrows kept them away from the river. As a result of this the Greek generals gathered together on the right of the line for a meeting with Pausanias. But they were even more concerned by the fact that they had no food left and that the supply columns from the Peloponnese were cut off by the Persian cavalry and could not reach their positions.

A decision was taken to move to a piece of land known as 'The Island' if the Persians did not launch a full-scale attack that day. The Island was closer to the city of Plataea and over a mile (about 2 km) from their present position by the spring of Gargaphia and the river Asopus. This inland island is formed by two branches of a river that flows down from Mount Cithaeron. At the widest point these channels are about six hundred yards (550 m) apart and they join together again further downstream. The Greeks planned to take up position there so that they would have a plentiful water supply and some protection from the Persian cavalry attacks which were causing them so much trouble in their present position.

It was agreed that they should do this in the middle of the night so that the Persians would not see them moving off and ruin the manoeuvre by sending the cavalry after them. When they reached the Island they intended to send half their force up on Mount Cithaeron to bring down the supply convoys which were cut off there.

It is difficult to imagine the Greeks and the Persians facing each other inactively for so long. The Greeks were vulnerable on both flanks and Mardonius should not have needed to wait eight days or more and for the advice of a Theban before using his cavalry to exploit this. Perhaps Herodotus confused the dates for the whole campaign, from the time the Peloponnesians set off for Boeotia, with the dates for the battle itself. Mardonius may have been hoping that the Greek alliance would break up. The story about Alexander's visit to the Athenian camp could, in fact, conceal a final attempt to persuade the Athenians to change sides. But general harassment by the cavalry and pressure on the Greeks' lines of supply were effective psychological weapons which Mardonius would not have delayed using.

Alexander's warning cannot have been of much value to the Greeks as they must have been in a constant state of readiness since first moving onto the ridge. In any case Mardonius did not launch a full-scale attack on the following day. However, he did succeed in pushing the Greeks off the ridge. The opportunities presented by this withdrawal and the probable detachment of a large force of hoplites to regain control of the supply routes were exactly what Mardonius needed. On the other hand, the manoeuvre might also give Pausanias the opportunity he was looking for. If it provoked a full-scale Persian attack, his hoplites could meet the enemy on terms that suited them best, if he could get them back and ready for battle in time.

THIRD PHASE

The Persian cavalry had harried the Greeks continually and did not break off until evening. Then, at the agreed hour that night, most of the Greeks moved off but with no intention of going to the agreed new position. Instead, delighted to be moving out of reach of the Persian cavalry, they retreated towards the city of Plataea until they reached the temple of Hera which is just outside the walls and about two and a half miles (4 km) from the spring of Gargaphia. There they halted.

When he saw the rest of the Greeks on their way, Pausanias ordered the Lacedaemonians to move off and follow the others, thinking they were all going to the new position as agreed. But one Spartan commander refused to obey this order. His name was Amompharetus and he refused to retreat in the face of the barbarians; he said that would be a disgrace to Sparta. He could not understand what was going on because he had not been at the council at which the decision to move back had been taken. Pausanias was angry at his disobedience but could not risk leaving Amompharetus and his men behind because they would certainly have been wiped out. So he kept the Lacedaemonians where they were and attempted to persuade Amompharetus that he was mistaken in what he was doing.

The Athenians also stayed where they were, knowing well the Spartans' habit of saying one thing and thinking something quite different. When the rest of the army had left and only they and the Spartans were in their original positions, the Athenians sent a horseman to ask Pausanias whether he was staying and what they should do. The Athenian messenger arrived to see Amompharetus picking up a boulder in the heat of the argument. He flung it at Pausanias' feet and said that was his voting pebble and he was voting against retreat! Pausanias told him he was a mad fool. The messenger asked his questions and Pausanias told him to tell the Athenians what was happening and request them to come over towards the Spartans' position and move off when they did.

The argument with Amompharetus went on till dawn and all that time Pausanias kept his men where they were. But then he gave the order for the rest of the Lacedaemonians and the Tegeans, who were with them, to move off along the foothills of Cithaeron. Pausanias thought Amompharetus would not stay behind once everyone else had gone, and he was quite right. The Athenians set off at the same time but followed a different route; they kept to the lower, level ground while the Lacedaemonians, in their fear of the Persian cavalry, clung to the skirts of Cithaeron.

Amompharetus thought Pausanias would not contemplate leaving him and his men, and he ordered them to stay where they were. But when he saw the rest of Pausanias' force on the move, he knew he really had been left behind. Then he ordered his men to march and led them at a steady pace in the same direction as the main force. The main force waited for him near a temple dedicated to Demeter by the river Moloeis. They stopped there, over a mile (about 2 km) away, so that they could go and help Amompharetus if he still did not move. But Amompharetus and his men joined them there at the very moment that the Persian cavalry attacked in full force. They had advanced to resume the attack and, finding the Greeks had abandoned their positions, pressed on until they caught up with them.

Pausanias knew that an attack by the Persian cavalry on any part of the Greek line while it was on the move could prove disastrous, so the manoeuvre had to be completed by early the following morning. He probably intended that the Island should be the centre of the new position since, if it was half a mile (600 m) wide, only a small proportion of the Greek line could fit into it. The ruins of Plataea on the left and perhaps the swell of Cithaeron at Hysiae on the right would protect the flanks and here the Greek line could safely be shortened, too, so that men could be sent to cover the main supply routes. Once in their new defensive postion the Greeks could wait and hope that the Persians would either attack them or run out of supplies and be forced to retreat.

The withdrawal obviously did not go according to plan but it is unlikely to have been as chaotic as Herodotus suggests. The Greeks from the centre probably did exactly as they were told. The following morning they were to provide the relief for the supply convoys. Pausanias' plan was that the Athenians should move over towards the Spartans as they retreated and join up with them along the new defensive line. In this shorter line he would have his two strongest hoplite contingents. It made sense to let the weaker, mixed centre retreat first.

The story of Amompharetus is obviously one told by other Greeks against the Spartans. It also puts the Athenians' failure to link up with the Spartans in the new position in a better light. Its source was, therefore, almost certainly Athenian! It is probable that Amompharetus, in fact, led a rearguard that covered the rest of the Spartans and enabled them to move back more rapidly and re-form in their new position. The Athenians had more ground to cover in moving from their position on the left of the ridge to the vicinity of the Island. Their failure to be where Pausanias wanted them to be when the Persians caught up with him was, perhaps, excusable

120

therefore, and would not have needed covering up if Athens and Sparta had not later become enemies. Keeping to the higher ground certainly did not save the Spartans from the Persian cavalry, so Herodotus' snide comment is not justified. In any case, Pausanias was simply following the most direct route from one position to the other and probably used the road.

THE LAST DAY

Mardonius immediately led the Persians across the Asopus at the double in pursuit of the Greeks, thinking they were running away. His objective was the Lacedaemonians and the Tegeans; they were the only Greeks he could see because the Athenians were concealed from him by the folds in the ground. When they saw the Persians starting off in pursuit of the Greeks, all the other contingents of the barbarian army raised their standards and immediately joined in the chase as fast as they could run. They were not organised in any way or in any sort of order, but simply streamed forward in a mass with a great deal of shouting. They were going to wipe the Greeks out.

When the cavalry attacked, Pausanias sent a horseman to the Athenians to ask them either to come and help him in full force or, if that was not possible, to send their archers. When they received this message, the Athenians moved at once, intending to give the Lacedaemonians the best support they could. But they could not complete the movement because they were attacked by the Greeks, fighting on the King's side, who had been positioned opposite them in the order of battle. They could not help the Lacedaemonians at all because they were fully committed themselves. So the Lacedaemonians and the Tegeans faced the Persians alone (50,000 Lacedaemonians and 3,000 Tegeans altogether, counting hoplites and light-armed men). They sacrificed to see if the time was right for them to attack and the omens were not good. The Persians had made a barricade from their wicker shields and were showering them with arrows from behind it, killing many and wounding even more. The Spartans were hard pressed and still the omens were bad. Then Pausanias looked towards the temple of Hera at Plataea and prayed to the goddess, begging her not to let them down.

As Pausanias prayed, the Tegeans rushed forward and charged the barbarians. And, at that moment, the sacrifices produced favourable omens. Then the Lacedaemonians charged as well and the Persians put away their bows and met their charge. At first the fighting was at the barricade. That went down. Then the barbarians grabbed the Greeks' spears and broke them, and there was a long and fierce hand-to-hand struggle by the temple of Demeter. The Persians were as strong and brave as the Greeks, but they were less well-armed, less skilful fighters and had less tactical sense. They hurled themselves against the Spartan line one by one, in tens, and in larger and smaller groups, and were cut down.

The Persians were most successful at whatever point in the line Mardonius was fighting, riding a white horse and leading his thousand Immortals. As long as Mardonius was alive the Persians held their ground, defended themselves and killed many Lacedaemonians. But when Mardonius and the men who fought beside him, the cream of the Persian army, were killed, the rest began to give way and fall back. What they suffered from most of all was their lack of armour; they were light-armed soldiers battling against hoplites.

So, that day the Spartans got their payment from Mardonius and avenged Leonidas, and Pausanias, son of Cleombrotus, won the most glorious victory ever witnessed by man. The defeated Persians retreated in disorder to their camp and the shelter of the wooden palisade which they had built in Theban territory.

Artabazus had disapproved from the start of the King's decision to leave Mardonius behind in Greece, and he was also angry that his advice against fighting had been ignored. At this point in the battle he turned and ran with the 40,000 men under his command, not to the palisade or the shelter of Thebes' city walls but straight to Phocis, with the aim of getting to the Hellespont as fast as he could.

The Greeks on the King's side made no effort to fight well, except for the Boeotians, who had a long battle with the Athenians. The Thebans amongst them fought particularly hard and lost 300 of their best men. But eventually the Boeotians were beaten. They did not follow the Persians and the great mass of their other allies, who had not struck a blow or played any useful part in the battle, but retreated to Thebes.

It is clear to me that everything depended on the Persians as far as the barbarians were concerned, because all the others turned and ran before they had even joined the battle when they saw the Persians in retreat. Only the cavalry, the Boeotian

122

cavalry and the rest, continued to face the enemy, helping their friends by covering their withdrawal.

The victorious Greeks gave chase, killing as they went. The retreat became a rout and the Greeks who were positioned away from the main battle around the temple of Hera heard about Pausanias' victory. Then they moved forward in no order. One force, following the Corinthians, kept to the foothills and made straight for the temple of Demeter. A second force grouped round the Megarians kept to the level ground and moved across the plain. The Theban cavalry saw this second force rushing forward in complete disorder, charged and killed six hundred, driving the rest back towards Cithaeron, an ignominious end.

The Persians and the rest managed to reach their camp and man the parapets before the Lacedaemonians got there. They did what they could to strengthen the defences and then when the Lacedaemonians arrived, fierce fighting broke out. Until the Athenians arrived, the Persians defended themselves well and had very much the upper hand because the Lacedaemonians were unskilled in siege warfare. But when the Athenians came up the fighting grew fiercer and continued for a long time. But eventually, through courage and determination, the Athenians succeeded in storming the ramparts and breaching them. Then the Greeks poured in. The Tegeans were the first inside and plundered Mardonius' tent. Amongst the spoils was the solid bronze manger from which Mardonius' horses fed, a spectacular trophy. (The Tegeans dedicated this to Athene but they shared everything else they won, like all the other Greeks.)

Once the defences were breached the barbarian army fell apart. There was no more thought of resistance – just panic and terror amongst the thousands trapped in that narrow space. In the slaughter that followed less than 3,000 out of 260,000 survived. On the Greek side 91 Spartans, 17 Tegeans and 52 Athenians died

In the barbarian army the Sacae were the cavalry who fought best while the Persians were the best foot soldiers. Mardonius was the individual who fought most bravely. As for the Greeks, the Tegeans and the Athenians did very well, but the Lacedaemonians fought best of all. I say this because they fought against the strongest section of the barbarian army and defeated it.

Once Mardonius knew what was happening, he reacted fast. He and his Persians were quickly up on Pausanias' position

123

while his Greek troops crossed the river and the ridge further west, and attacked the Athenians in open ground behind the ridge and in front of Plataea and the Island. Two battles were taking place simultaneously, a mile apart. On the left it was a local affair, Greek against Greek, and a conventional hoplite engagement. On the right the real issue was being settled. The rest of the Persian army was streaming up behind Mardonius, some of it making for the gap between the Athenians and the Spartans. The rest of the Greeks are more likely to have advanced now to fill this gap than later, as Herodotus suggests, to join in the rout. Their action may not have been very orderly; a number of relatively small contingents, each with its own general, would not have been well co-ordinated in a spontaneous movement. but it certainly was not 'ignominious'. By keeping the Theban cavalry occupied it may have made an important contribution to the Athenians' victory and it may also have helped Pausanias by guarding his left flank.

Herodotus does not explain why the Persians stopped and set up their shield-wall in a line in front of the Spartans. It was exactly the confrontation that Mardonius had spent the past few days avoiding and that the Greeks had hoped to bring about. Mardonius probably did not expect to be met by a solid hoplite line. If Herodotus is correct about the large numbers of light-armed troops with the Spartans, they may have extended Pausanias' line so far that a flanking movement was not possible. The hoplite line would have been well over half a mile long and, with screens of light-armed men on each flank, Pausanias' force could have covered more ground than Mardonius'. Also, Pausanias used the omens from sacrifices to justify delaying his attack while the arrows rained down until he saw that the Persians were too deeply massed to give way before his charge. Then he gave the order and the result was never in doubt, even before Mardonius had died his hero's death.

Herodotus' casualty figures must be treated with the same caution as all his statistics. The Persian losses would certainly have been heavy and the Greeks' relatively light. But the 40,000 men who escaped with Artabazus might have been a quarter or even a third of Mardonius' total force at Plataea. The immense slaughter in the Persian camp may have been mainly imagined. The cover provided by the cavalry could have allowed a large number of the more mobile Asian troops to escape completely. On the other hand the figures for the Greeks seem to take no account of the occasions when

Herodotus suggests they were sustaining heavy losses. They do not even include the 600 Greeks who were, according to Herodotus, ridden down by the Theban cavalry. But, whatever the casualties, the victory was overwhelming and decisive. The Persian War in mainland Greece was over. It was a Spartan victory and Pausanias' generalship was crucial in it. The victory also owed a lot to the determination and strong, if temporary, unity of the Greek alliance as a whole.

SPOILS OF VICTORY

After the battle Pausanias gave orders that no-one was to touch the spoils and had everything collected up by the helots. They moved through the camp and found tents and the furniture in them encrusted with gold and silver; they found golden flasks, goblets and dishes; and they found wagons loaded with sacks full of gold and silver vases. They stripped the dead of their gold bracelets, necklaces and daggers, and hardly bothered with their fine, richly coloured clothing. The helots stole a lot and sold it to the Aeginetans, though there was much that they could not hide. The Aeginetans laid the foundations for their great wealth on this occasion by buying gold from the helots at the price of bronze!

When it had all been gathered together, a tenth of it was dedicated to Apollo at Delphi, a tenth to Zeus at Olympia and a tenth to Poseidon at the Isthmus. The rest was divided, each Greek taking a share of the Persians' concubines, gold, silver and oxen according to his entitlement. I could not find out how much was set aside for the men who distinguished themselves most in the battle, but I think they were all rewarded. For Pausanias ten times as much was set aside as for anyone else – women, horses, bullion, camels, everything.

There is a story that Xerxes left all his campaigning equipment in Greece with Mardonius. When Pausanias saw his tent, decorated with gold and silver and bright tapestries, he ordered Mardonius' chefs and pastry cooks to prepare him dinner as they would for Mardonius. They obeyed and Pausanias was amazed at the sight of the beautifully covered gold and silver couches and the magnificent banquet they had prepared for him. He thought it would be amusing to have his own servants prepare him a Spartan dinner. This was done and Pausanias, roaring with laughter at the great difference between the two meals, sent for the Greek generals. They came and Pausanias said, 'My friends –

I have called you here so that I can show you how foolish the commander of the Persians was. He lived in such luxury yet came to Greece to take our poverty from us!'

When they had divided the spoils, the Greeks buried their dead. Then they held a council. They agreed to march on Thebes and order the Thebans to hand over those who were chiefly responsible for their alliance with Persia. They arrived outside the city eleven days after the battle, devastated the surrounding countryside and attacked the walls. The siege lasted for three weeks and then the men the Greeks most wanted offered to give themselves up. They thought they would be put on trial and expected to bribe themselves out of trouble. But Pausanias suspected that this was what they had in mind. So, as soon as they had been handed over, he sent the allied army home, took his prisoners to Corinth and had them executed.

11 Final victory

MYCALE IN IONIA

On the very same day as the battle of Plataea the Persians suffered as crushing a defeat at Mycale in Ionia. A secret deputation from Samos had come to the Greek fleet while it was stationed at Delos and persuaded the generals that the Greeks only had to show themselves to make the Ionians revolt and the Persians withdraw or, if they stayed, prove the richest prize the Greeks had ever won.

The omens were good and the Greeks sailed from Delos to Samos. Off Samos they prepared for battle, but the Persians knew they were coming and the whole fleet sailed to the mainland except for the Phoenicians, who were sent off in a different direction. The Persians had decided not to risk a battle at sea because they thought they would be no match for the Greeks. They sailed to the mainland instead and to the protectioɪ of the army of 60,000 which was there at Mycale. Tigranes, the best looking and tallest man in Persia, was in command of it with orders from Xerxes to watch over Ionia.

The Persians came to Mycale, beached their ships and built a wall of tree trunks and boulders around them. Then they surrounded the wall with sharpened stakes and made preparations to withstand a siege or win a victory. When the Greeks discovered that the barbarians had slipped away to the mainland, they were annoyed and at first could not decide between going back to Delos and sailing to the Hellespont. In the end they decided to do neither of these things but to sail to the mainland. So they got everything ready for a sea-battle, the boarding ladders and all the other things they would need, and made for Mycale. When they approached the Persian position no ships came out to meet them. They saw the whole fleet beached behind the wall and a large force drawn up along the shore in battle order. Leutychides, the Spartan commanding the Greeks, sailed his ship as close in as he could and, using a herald, gave this message to the Ionians. 'Listen to this, all who can hear; the Persians will not understand a word of it. When the battle begins, think of your freedom and remember our code word – Hera. You who can hear me, pass this message on to those who cannot.' Leutychides was trying to do what Themistocles had attempted to do after Artemisium: either the barbarians would know nothing about the message but it would win over the Ionians, or they would find out about it and distrust their Greek allies.

After Leutychides had delivered his message the Greeks beached their ships, disembarked and formed their battle line. When the Persians saw them preparing to attack and heard how they had encouraged the Greeks on their side to desert, they disarmed the Samians because they suspected them of supporting the Greeks. The Persians also sent the Milesians off to guard the passes leading down from the mountains behind Mycale. They gave as their reason for doing this the Milesians' knowledge of the terrain, but they really wanted to keep them away from the rest of the army. The Persians took these measures to protect themselves from the Ionians whom they expected to turn against them if they had the opportunity; then they went to their positions and set up their shield-wall.

When they were ready, the Greeks advanced. At that moment, a rumour passed through the ranks that a great victory had been won over Mardonius in Boeotia and a herald's staff was found at the water's edge. Divine intervention in human affairs shows itself in many ways and especially in this – the victory at Plataea fell on the same day as the victory that was about to be won at Mycale, and the rumour of the first victory reached the Greeks at Mycale in time to lift their spirits and strengthen their courage for the battle they were about to fight. Both Greeks and barbarians were eager for battle, in fact, because both sides knew that the Hellespont and the Ionian islands were the prize they were fighting for.

The Athenians and those positioned next to them, about half the Greek line altogether, moved forward along the beach and the level ground behind it. But the Lacedaemonians and the rest had to pick their way across a gully and some hills. Well before the Lacedaemonians had completed this manoeuvre, the Athenians and the rest of the army were engaged. The Persians defended themselves successfully for as long as their shield-wall held. But then the Athenians and the other Greeks with them urged each other on to make the victory their own and not share it with the Lacedaemonians. Then they increased their efforts and changed the course of the battle. They burst through the shields and charged into the Persian ranks. The Persians held the Greeks at first and kept up this resistance for some time. But eventually they fell back behind their fortifications.

The Athenians, the Corinthians, the Sicyonians and the Troezenians followed close behind and forced their way into the camp. Once their defences had been broken through, the barbarians put up no further resistance but turned and ran, all except the Persians. They continued to fight in small groups as the Greeks streamed into the camp. Two of the Persian generals managed to escape but two were killed; Tigranes was one of the latter. The Persians were still fighting when the Lacedaemonians and the rest of the army arrived on the scene in time to help finish them off. Many Greeks also died in the battle.

The Samians in the Persian army who had been disarmed did what they could to help the Greeks, seeing from the start that the battle could swing either way. The other Ionians followed the Samians' example and turned on the Persians. The Milesians had been sent up into the passes above Mycale to guard them and to be ready to act as guides if the Persians needed to escape in that direction, as well as to separate them from the rest of the army. In fact the Milesians guided the escaping Persians along tracks which led them back into the arms of their enemies and then joined in the killing themselves.

This battle marked the second Ionian revolt against the Persians. The Greeks who distinguished themselves most in it were the Athenians. The few barbarians who escaped after the battle managed to get over the mountains behind Mycale and back to Sardis.

> The battle of Mycale was fought between much smaller forces than the battle of Plataea. The Greek fleet may not have consisted of many more than the 110 ships that had assembled at Aegina earlier in the year. The alliance could not spare many men, either light-armed soldiers to row or hoplites to fight on deck, while Mardonius was in Greece. But it was necessary to counter any threat of a new sea-borne attack on Greece; and this time the Samians had persuaded the Greeks that attack was the best means of doing this. Each trireme had twenty or thirty hoplites on board and some of the oarsmen may also have had weapons with them and taken part in the battle. So perhaps 6,000 Greeks disembarked to attack the Persians and their unsteady allies.

The Persian fleet without the Phoenicians was probably about equal in strength or perhaps weaker. No explanation for the departure of the Phoenicians is known; they may have been sent to another part of the coast to guard against revolt there. Tigranes would have had a few thousand men with him, not tens of thousands. The Persian army was small enough to be defeated by just two or three thousand Greeks (the half of the total force that advanced along the shore). But the fact that the Persians initially took on the Greeks in front of their fortifications suggests they might have comfortably outnumbered them at this stage.

The story of rumours of victory at Plataea encouraging the Greeks is probably no more than a pleasing invention. Even, in Herodotus' eyes, it seems, Mycale was a lightweight affair in comparison with Plataea. But its consequences were important. It did not secure freedom from Persia for the Greeks of Asia but it did secure the Aegean and the grain-carrying sealanes down from the Black Sea for the European Greeks. This was particularly important for the Athenians whose naval and economic strength was to grow so rapidly in the years that followed. It was their reason for campaigning in the Chersonese well into that autumn after the Peloponnesians had gone home.

AFTER MYCALE

With the Persian invasion force defeated on land and driven out of Greece, the Athenians no longer needed to place themselves under the supreme command of the Spartans or to bargain with them. Shortly after Mycale the Athenians and the Peloponnesians began to go their separate ways. The Athenians continued to campaign in the Chersonese because they were looking beyond the immediate military objective of destroying the Persian bridges over the Hellespont, which must have been replaced in the spring, if they were there at all in 479.

When the fighting was over the Greeks took everything of value out of the camp and burned the Persian ships and the wall surrounding them. Then they sailed to Samos. There they held a council and debated whether they should evacuate the Ionians to Greece and abandon Ionia to the barbarians. It was felt that there was no possibility of protecting the Ionians from the Persians indefinitely. But without protection the Ionians had no hope of escaping punishment. The Peloponnesians favoured expelling the Greeks who had given in to the Persians from their cities and settling the Ionians in their place. But the Athenians were against the idea and felt the Peloponnesians had no right to decide on the fate of Athenian colonists. They argued their case very forcefully and the Peloponnesians gave way. Samos, Chios and Lesbos, and other islands that had fought alongside them were brought into the Greek alliance and swore solemnly to be loyal to it and never to leave it.

Then the Greeks set sail for the Hellespont intending to destroy the bridges which they expected to find still in place. When they reached Abydos and found the bridges gone, the Peloponnesians went home. But the Athenians decided to stay and try an attack on the Chersonese. So they sailed over from Abydos and besieged Sestos. This was the most strongly fortified city in the area and all the people from the surrounding towns had moved in for protection when they heard the Greeks had come to the Hellespont.

The siege went on into the autumn and the Athenians began to long for home. They were depressed at their failure to capture the city and begged the generals to take them home. But the generals would not do this until either the city fell or the Athenian assembly recalled them, and the Athenians accepted their decision. Inside the walls things were very bad; the people were even reduced to boiling their bedstraps for food. When even this ran out all the Persians climbed over the fortifications at the back of the city and escaped through the weakest sector of the Greek lines during the night. Next day the people of the Chersonese signalled to the Greeks that the Persians had gone, and opened the gates. Some of the Greeks occupied the city but most of them pursued the Persians, caught up with them and, after a long fight, killed some and took the rest prisoner. Amongst the prisoners was Artayctes, one of the Persian generals. He had governed the Chersonese for Xerxes and ruled it with evil cunning, robbing tombs and desecrating temples. The people of the Chersonese demanded that he be put to death and Xanthippus, the Athenian general, agreed. So they took Artayctes out to the headland which had been Xerxes' bridgehead into Europe and crucified him and stoned his son to death before his eyes.

After this the Greeks sailed home with their spoils, which included the great cables from Xerxes' bridges. They dedicated these to the gods and that ended the year's campaigning.

The Persian War was at an end. The Greeks continued to fight against the Persians for the next thirty years in Cyprus and Egypt and on the northern shores of the eastern Mediterranean. There were both victories and defeats. But in the defence of their home territory and of their way of life, the Greeks had won an absolute victory. This victory did not belong only to the hoplites, the Greeks who mattered most on the battlefield and off it. It also belonged to the more humble citizens who sweated, naked at their oars or served on land as light-armed soldiers or in the supply lines.

All through the war, as Herodotus clearly shows, Greek unity was precarious and very fragile. The alliance was breaking up within weeks of Plataea. But in battle the Greeks were very strongly united by shared ideals and a grim determination to preserve their world in which these ideals could be achieved. The Persians could not see this strength behind the more obvious but less important local rivalries and clashes of interest, or they underestimated it.

In 478 Athens took over the leadership of the Greeks against the Persians. Soon Athenians were fighting against Greeks who had been their allies. This was not because they had become allies of the Persians, but because they did not want to be part of the alliance on which Athens was rapidly tightening her grip. This alliance was soon to become the Athenian empire and the source of the wealth and the confidence, security and pride without which Athenian civilisation could not have flowered as it did. A collision with the other major Greek alliance, the Peloponnesians with Sparta at their head, was inevitable. Twenty years after Mycale and Plataea and ten years before peace was formally made between Persia and the Greeks, the Peloponnesian war began its first phase.

At the beginning of his history of the Peloponnesian war, the historian Thucydides took up the story almost exactly where Herodotus left off. According to Thucydides, looking back at the Persian War, the Corinthians claimed that 'the main reason for the barbarians' failure was their own mistakes'. There is a good deal of truth in this. The Persians' main mistake was to attempt to extend their influence westwards by direct, military action. Diplomacy, subversion and gold had already proved themselves highly effective weapons. In time, they might have been successful in the whole of Greece and failure would certainly have been far less costly.

To this major miscalculation the Persians added an important strategic and tactical misjudgement. Their best troops were no match for hoplites in the kind of static battle that hoplite tactics were developed for. As Herodotus points out, the most heavily-armed Persians and Medes were 'light-armed' by Greek standards and weight of numbers was no compensation in frontal attacks; Thermopylae and then Plataea conclusively demonstrated this. The Persians would have done much better to make their attack more exclusively a naval operation. Their fleet was larger, their ships were better and, particularly in the Phoenicians, they had much greater resources of skill and experience. Used independently rather than in combination with the army, the Persian navy could well have won Greece for Xerxes.

Whatever the rights and wrongs of the Persians' strategy, their invasion of Greece with such a large army was a remarkable feat, and its objectives were very nearly achieved. The sea-battles of Artemisium and Salamis were very closely contested (the Greeks expected to have to fight again at Salamis) and, until the final day, the Persians were winning the battle of Plataea. If Mardonius had been able to restrain himself, or if Pausanias had not managed the manoeuvres during that last night (the manoeuvres which he was able to control) so well, the outcome might have been very different. The Persians came too close to succeeding for their failure to be attributed only to the mistakes they made.

Herodotus seems to end his account rather abruptly. But by the end of 479 the war was effectively over with the lifting of any direct Persian threat. However, Herodotus rounds off his history with a brief anecdote which, for him, perhaps summed up the Persians' failure:

Artayctes' grandfather once suggested that the Persians should move out of their 'small, rough land' and go and live somewhere better. There was plenty of good land nearby and much more further off. He argued that the Persians would become even more famous if they occupied another country and that this was a natural move for a race of rulers to make. Now was the time to act when Persia had so many peoples and all of Asia in her power.

Cyrus, who was then King, was not impressed by the idea. 'If you do this', he said, 'be prepared to be subjects rather than rulers. Soft land rears soft men. Rich crops and good fighters do not grow in the same soil.'

Passages translated

Most of the following passages are translated in their entirety. In some there are slight abridgements or alterations to Herodotus' original sequence. In a few places it was necessary to introduce a sentence or two to link passages more smoothly.

1 The Ionian Revolt
Aristagoras and Histiaeus: V.35–7.
Athens and Sparta: V.49; V.55: V.78; V.97.
The burning of Sardis: V.100–2; VI.18; VI.21; VI.42.
Mardonius' expedition: VI.43–5.

2 Marathon
The second Persian expedition: VI.48–9; VI.94–5; VI.97; VI.99–106.
The battle: VI.108–17.
After the battle: VI.120; VI.132; VI.136; VII.1; VII.4–7.

3 The eclipse of Greece
Debate and decision: VII.8–10.
Preparations: VII.20–2; VII.24; VII.31–2; VII.34–8; VII:40.
Abydos: VII.44–50; VII.53–6.
Xerxes' army and fleet: VII.60–1; VII.64; VII.82–4.
Damaratus: VII.101–5.

4 Face your doom!
Greek reactions: VII.131–3; VII.138.
Athens and the Delphic oracle: VII.139–42.
Themistocles: VII.143–4.
The Greek alliance: VII.145–7.
Northern Greece: VII.172–5.
First line of defence: VII.176–8.
First blood: VII.179–87.
Boreas: VII.188–91.
First encounter at Artemisium: VII.192–5.

5 A fallen king
Thermopylae: VII.201–10.
The battle begins: VII.210–12.
Second day: VII.212–17.
Third day: VII.217–26; VII.228; VII.233.
The next move: VII.234–8.

6 The foundation-stone of freedom
Artemisium: VIII.1–8.
The battle begins: VIII.9–13.
Second day: VIII.14.
Third day: VIII.15–19; VIII.21–6.

7 Blessed island
Salamis: VIII.40–3; VIII.49–50.
The fall of Athens: VIII.51–5.
Themistocles' strategy: VIII.57–62.
Xerxes decides: VIII.66; VIII.68–70.
Themistocles chooses his moment: VIII.70–2; VIII.74–6; VIII.78–82.

8 A wooden wall
The battle of Salamis: VIII.83–100.
After the battle: VIII.107–12.
Aeschylus' 'The Persians': 210–14; 233–46; 249–53; 266–7; 272–9; 284–5; 331–2.

9 Autumn 480 to Spring 479
Autumn 480: VIII.113–14; VIII.121; VIII.123–5.
Winter: VIII.136; VIII.140–4.
Spring 479: IX.1–13; IX.15; IX.19; VIII.131–2.

10 The battle of Plataea
First phase: IX.20–6.
Second phase: IX.33; IX.36–7; IX.38–42; IX.44–6; IX.49–51.
Third phase: IX.52–7.
The last day: IX.59–64; IX.66–71.
Spoils of victory: IX.80–3; IX.86–8.

11 Final victory
Mycale in Ionia: IX.90; IX.96–105.
After Mycale: IX.106; IX.114–15; IX.117–21; IX.122.

Index

Printed in the United States
By Bookmasters